The Barack Obama Juncture and Other Emphases on the Mind and the Fate of Human Society

Christian Awogbade

This book is also published under the title: The Reason We Act the Way We Do Is That We Are Not Intelligent Enough to Act Otherwise

Copyright © 2016 Christian Awogbade

All rights reserved.

DEDICATION

We will never know if the <u>best</u> person is the best person, or if he should think that he is the best person.

It is highly unlikely anyway that a person would have a useful and sustaining reason to think that he is the best.

In any case, to let those who are determined to impose themselves dictate society's values is like to let the fellow who is barreling down the highway in the rain and in suspect visibility think that he belongs on a pedestal.

This book is dedicated to anyone who has ever tried at anything. This book is dedicated to the people whom the world never know, the giants who walk the face of the earth unnoticed.

CONTENTS

ACKNOWLEDGMENTS I

1 INTRODUCTION 1

2 ON COEXISTING 5

3 ON WHAT IS RIGHT 63

4 ON WHAT IS BEAUTIFUL 91

5 ON WHAT IS BEYOND 111

6 ON KNOWING 127

7 NOTES 143

ACKNOWLEDGMENTS

A word of thanks to the people who are the source of my inspiration. To family and friends, thank you. Thank you to those who make the music that I listen to, the music that take me else where. A special thanks to those whose music I listen to in awe: Earl Klugh, Michael Franks, Miles Davis, King Sunny Ade.

1 INTRODUCTION

The only struggle we are in is the one with our minds, each of us, individually, with no one else involved.

Selah!

One day, I watched Franklin Graham in an exchange with a television panel. In the conversation, which was about Barack Obama and Rick Santorum, Franklin Graham essentially said this: *I believe a person is a Christian when he tells me that he is. Both Rick Santorum and Barack Obama have told me that they are Christians. I am convinced that Rick Santorum is a Christian. I am not convinced that Barack Obama is a Christian*[1].

Late one night, I was driving down the interstate in very foggy conditions. This was only a few days after the horrific multiple vehicle accident on interstate 75 in Florida that claimed so many lives; the one that may have been caused by heavy fog. As soon as I started driving into the banks of fog, that accident in Florida was the first thing that came to my mind. For me, it was time to be more careful. It was time for an extra layer of alertness and preparedness. I found myself fully engaged, employing all measures of safety, including traveling at what I considered to be safe speed relative to the visibility.

In my 'careful' state, I was surprised that there were people driving faster than I, and that vehicles were passing mine. I started to ponder the situation, questioning the judgment of the drivers who were going faster than I was. I became an arbiter, which I believe was my right based on my own good driving record. How could these people be so careless? How could they be so irresponsible? Were they not aware of the Florida accident, and how it was caused by fog? How it could have been avoided? I began to get riled up. I got madder and madder at every passing 'thoughtless' and 'unskilled' driver who, in my opinion, did not deserve to own much less operate an automobile. As this state consumed me, it occurred to me that I myself had just passed a vehicle. At that moment, I wondered if the person I passed thought of me what I had been thinking of the people who passed me.

I have concluded for reasons that may be inherent in the two stories that I have shared and many more that I will be sharing in this book that we should consider engaging our minds, in ways more important than focusing on what is right and what is wrong, what is good and what is evil, what is moral and what is immoral, etc. In fact, it seems evident that we are incapable of this sort of reconciliation anyway. We have trouble with it, with interpretation, with where to draw the lines, as well as with inconsistencies in the principles that we attempt to put forth in establishing our standards once we focus on pitching one thought against another. Unfortunately, this creates what I consider to be a Double Error Effect, whereby we take a potentially wrong approach to a problem and then find ourselves using an incapable mind to work on a puzzle that is already off course.

When I was younger, I always thought it would be possible for the mind to become advanced enough that a person would actually have trouble saying something that made no sense – something that the person knew made no sense. I thought that a person would not be able to bring himself to that point(of saying something nonsensical - something the person himself already thought, by own standards, was unreasonable) because he would be overrun by the desire for and pursuit of something useful. I am much older now, and I have thought of things that may need to fill the gap between the mental flights of my youth and what a capable adult mind might understand. I think of my early concept of an advanced mind in a way that it teaches me, for instance, that there always at the very least has to be a **Useful Starting Point.** Now, as an adult, I acknowledge that not mistaking a camera for a golf club is a good start for me. I consider the notion that not going south on I-75 toward Miami when one intends to go north toward Valdosta is a useful starting point. It would be an important starting point for a capable mind, for instance, not to assume an opposing viewpoint just for the sake of disagreeing with a person. I consider such an event a useful starting point.

Something else that comes to mind in my journey toward a mind that works is that there has to be the presence of an unceasing **Internal Dialogue.** In recognizing that I may never engage my mind or that I may never ask myself a single question about anything now, in a week, in a month, in ten years, I now must not only make the effort to ponder things, but I also must carry on this internal exercise as if I had people around the table who were affording me other perspectives on an ongoing dialogue. For me, a reminder is that I once asked coworkers to guess why I would not steal from my job. One of the answers that I got was maybe I was a nice guy. Some people suggested that maybe I was afraid of getting caught and losing my job. Some people suggested that stealing went against my religious convictions. Some people simply said that I deemed it immoral. However, these answers were not the reason I would not steal from my job. In fact, these were all reasons that I had considered at one time or another as a result of my internal dialogue on the matter. As if my friends were there to carry on these conversations with me, day after day I pondered, adopting reasons along the way that I would soon discard after further questioning. This continued for a period of time until I concluded that the reason I did not steal is that it was not in my job description. The presence of an internal dialogue forces me to continue to examine my position on why I would not steal from an employer, if only to be sure that I am still comfortable with where I stand.

Ultimately, I do not have to have a mind that works. I do not have to work at it. I do not have to try. If I never knew where milk came from, it would not be the end of the world; only I would not know **What is Possible.** If it never occurs to me that the direction in which I point the car determines if and when I get home, or if a kitchen spatula is what I consider the right tool with which to hit a golf ball, it is not the end of the world. Only I will not know what is possible. If a person buys a camera and never discovers the extent of the camera's capabilities beyond knowing how to snap a picture, it will not be the end of the world. If the camera can take photos at night at a high speed and in cloudy weather and make it look like a bright sunny day but the owner of the camera never finds out, we may say that he has not gotten his money's worth. However, that is where it ends. The only currency we have is the thought of what is possible. If we never ask ourselves another question, if we never begin an internal dialogue, if we never look for a useful starting point in the hope that there is something that always follows, if I decide to be intellectually idle, which can be done, if I never care to find out who is innocent and who is guilty, if I do not labor to help find a cure for a terminal disease, if we fail to find that the earth is whatever shape it is, it will not be because we are good or evil, rich or poor, technologically advanced or not, pious or otherwise. If we never care to pursue what is possible, it will not be because there is good or there is evil or there is right or there is wrong or there is rich or there is poor or there is moral or there is immoral. If we never bring ourselves to pursue what is possible, it will be for an entirely different reason.

2 ON COEXISTING

The reason we act the way we do is that we are not intelligent enough to act otherwise.

One day in the early 2000s, I watched a man try to keep a door open. I stood there and watched him apply a door stop to the back of the door. He did this and as he let go, he watched the door drop and slam shut. Again and again, this man applied the wedge from the back of the door. Finally, on the fourth try, he shoved the wedge in from the front and was able to hold the door open.

While witnessing this series of events, I thought three things. The first thing I thought was that if the man was going to keep the door open, it would not be by applying the wedge to the back of the door. The second thing that I thought was that if the man did not begin to pay attention to what he was doing, he could be at it a while. The last thing I thought was that this man and his attempt to keep a door open is nothing more than a condition, an adventure toward what is possible.

Since this experience, I have seen the world in a light similar to one where a man applies a door stop to the back of the door. I realized at the time that I could not have looked at this man and said, "If only he were a rocket scientist, he would not have done that." I knew then, as I know now, that I could not have looked at the man and said, "If he had money, that would have prevented his condition." I was left to think that the reason a man would keep applying a wedge to the back of a door is that he was not thinking about it; he had not paid enough attention to become intelligent enough to act differently.

In the world, in this world where we find ourselves in all sorts of conditions, the reason we handle things the way we do, the reason we act the way we do is not that we are doctors or lawyers or garbage collectors or hotel operators. The reason we act the way we do is that we are not intelligent enough to act otherwise. As such, our job as human beings, really, is not to become doctors and lawyers and philanthropists and heads of states and professional athletes. These are 'side jobs.' **Our job as human beings is to think – to have a framework for thinking – because this determines what sort of doctors and lawyers and Supreme Court justices and business operators and law enforcement officers we become.**

The reason we act the way we do is not that we are smart or that we are dumb or that we know the difference between good and evil or that we can define good and evil or that we are right or that we are wrong or that we are rich or that we are poor or that we went to school or that we did not go to school or that we live in a technologically advanced society or that we live in a hut in a remote part of the world. The reason we act the way we do is that we are not intelligent enough to act otherwise.

Though I understand that thinking is an interest of mine, something that I enjoy doing, the same way that a person might enjoy hiking, we have to stop here and talk about something. This is definitely one of those "useful starting point" moments. We have to agree on something. What we have to agree on is that thinking is not like hiking. Thinking is not like hiking in the sense that I do not have to like hiking or hike. However, a person who enjoys hiking does not have a choice; he has to like thinking. He has to participate in the act of thinking. Well, actually, he has a choice, but that will be evident later. In other words, and in the context of how and where our individual lives come into contact with those of other people, we have no choice but to participate – we should participate.

Thinking is different from hiking in that a person may not have to participate in hiking, but he may have to participate in thinking. Here is another example. I do not have to learn ballroom dancing, but I may want to learn how to drive. In a sense, though ballroom dancing can be a nice hobby for a person the same way that driving can be a fun hobby for a person, driving is different from ballroom dancing in that it can be a responsibility. It has a certain I-really-have-to-know-how-to-do-this dimension to it. This potentially constrains a person from wanting to say, "Forget it; I'm doing this my way. I'm checking out today. Forget all this driving stuff."

The reason we act the way we do is that we are not intelligent enough to act otherwise. The reason we are not intelligent enough to act otherwise is that we have not thought about it. Clearly, this is not the same as how we think about becoming a doctor, a head of state, a lawyer, a garbage collector, or a believer in one religion or another. The reason we act the way we do is that we are not intelligent enough to know that our level of intelligence affects what kind of doctor or what kind of head of state or what kind of garbage collector a person becomes.

The reason we act the way we do is that we are not intelligent enough to act otherwise; and the reason we are not intelligent enough to act otherwise is that we are not doing anything about becoming more intelligent, from individuals, to groups, to communities, to nations. The effort to become intelligent enough – to change from acting one way to acting a different way – is what we are lacking. As a result, our conversation should be about that. Our work, very simply, should be about how we can be more intelligent than we currently are.

Clearly, we will always be in one condition or another. We will always be in one outcome or another. In a way, it is worth acknowledging that conditions are not in themselves an end, they can change. Whether a man can keep a door open or not will not be the end of the world. However, because whether he can keep a door open or not – a condition – is a matter of where his mind is, it might become obvious to him that there are so many possibilities as far as the condition in which he finds himself with regards to keeping a door open is concerned. One of these conditions is that he applies a wedge to the back of a door. Another of these conditions is that he applies a wedge to the front of the door. Yet another condition is that he uses a completely different mechanism to keep a door open. **It is all a matter of where his mind is.**

Put differently, and as a matter of a useful starting point, we should be less interested in what a person has to say. I am less interested in what I have to say. These are conditions that change, or these are conditions that can change. Rather, we should be more interested in what framework, what body of knowledge, if any, a person claims and uses to generate the thoughts that he has, the beliefs that he espouses. Building up that framework, examining it constantly, holding town square conversations about it, is the driver for what outcomes we create – for whether we stand a chance of becoming more intelligent.

So, in a way, the condition of a man who shoves a wedge into the back of the door is like that of a man who, while he gets ready for work one early morning, thinks that he has picked out a pair of black pants. If we ask him, he may tell us that he has planned to wear a pair of black pants for the day. Of course, it is of no use what the man tells us about the color of his pants. Sooner or later, it becomes evident, perhaps when he steps into the light.

What these two individuals have in common is the reason that I have written this book. There is a gap between what we think, what we build up, what we make up, what we wish is, and what eventually prevails. We have a fundamental choice to bridge this gap. In any outcome that we are in, any condition, there will always be a 'veil' that separates us from what is possible. Of course, what we know is that how we use our minds determines what outcome or condition we create, beginning with whether we use our minds at all.

We often speak of accelerators. For instance, we speak of technology as an accelerator. We might soon find that the mind is the one thing we should desire, most of all, to accelerate. The mind is the only thing to accelerate because it will not matter how many people we are able to gather into a town square with a message sent with the push of a cell phone button. It will always only matter what they talk about.

The point that I am trying to make is this: If it turns out that the reason a man is heading toward a cliff on his motorcycle is that he has a piece of clothing caught in his face, we will be quick to offer that the solution is for him to remove the piece of clothing from his face. It will be less likely for us to consider, and I submit this as irony, that the man may not know that he sees no obstruction to his view. Put differently, the man may think that he sees where he is going.

Though I have said that the reason we act the way we do is that we are not intelligent enough to act otherwise, I recognize that some people may not agree with me. I recognize that the reason some may not agree with me is the same reason that we all, for the most part, myself included, always think that we are right. I do not think that we can blame a man who is heading for a cliff if, for whatever reason, all he sees is an on-ramp. **This reason is one that I refer to as The Mind Eyes Condition. I consider that this is a challenging condition in that the tool that we need to sort out the fact that everyone thinks he is right – the mind – is also the tool that needs sorting out. The tool that we need to use to get to clarity is the tool that needs clearing up.** And for anyone who is entertained so far, it appears that the next pressing thing is to ask, "How do we clear it up; how do we become more intelligent?"

How do we get the mind sorted out? How do we become more intelligent, perhaps so that we can get past the disagreements that you have had with me so far reading this book? Well, here is what I think about how to become more intelligent. What I think is that there is no handbook for it. There is no handbook that a person can purchase and study for a certification examination, so that we can pass him on the street and know that he has been designated as an intelligent person. What I think is that wanting to know how to become more intelligent is like wanting to know if the reason you are a big tipper is that the waiter is nice to you, or if the reason the waiter is nice to you is that you are a big tipper.

I submit to you that you actually may never know if the reason a person is nice to you is that you are a big tipper, or if the reason you tip a person well is for the outstanding service that you receive. The reason is that those two things actually have to happen in concert. I refer to it as **The Precedence Dynamic.** Another way to put it is to say that we will never know. We will never know because the only way to know if the reason a waiter is nice to me is that I am a big tipper is to test it. The only way to test if a person is nice to me because I tip well is not to tip well. Unfortunately, if I decide to stiff my waiter and the person becomes less than welcoming to me the next time, I will not be able to say that the reason the person is unfriendly is that I tipped well.

Another example that comes to mind is that of a couple in which one has given the other a deadline for an engagement. If a person decides that she has dated her boyfriend long enough and issues an ultimatum for marriage, we will never know if the reason the man goes forward with the wedding is that he intended to marry his girlfriend all along. We will only know that a wedding took place after an ultimatum was issued. Precisely, a bride will never know if the reason she is married is that her boyfriend intended to marry her, or that she gave him an ultimatum. There are two things that have to happen in concert: the first is that the two people do intend to marry each other; the second is that there are no ultimatums involved.

We cannot try to find out if we are intelligent or not because we will have to do something contrary to make that point. Unfortunately, by the time we do that, the condition will have changed. **For this reason, I have considered that the thought, the reason we act the way we do is that we are not intelligent enough to act otherwise, is an axiom.**

Years ago, I had a conversation with an associate about something that had been neglected. I am a hotel operator, and it was a cleanliness issue. I wanted to be clear that the associate found the neglect unacceptable. As I tried to make the point, the associate interjected that the reason for the oversight was that no one, given that the associate was fairly new at the time, had pointed it out in training. As I tried to empower the associate by making the point that the matter was not a hotel specific standard, essentially saying that the judgment required for the situation did not necessarily require hotel specific training, the associate continued to try to save face by saying that if I personally had taken the time to point out the issue, the standard would have been observed. There are two things that have to happen in concert here that will make for a useful starting point. The first is that the associate welcomes mistakes and does not let the lesson be lost in defending self – the intention going in has to be to want to do the best job. The second thing is that the hotel operator's purpose for the exchange has to be in making the most useful decision for the operation specific to the situation and nothing more.

If you decide to help a person in need two things will have to happen in concert. The two things that have to happen at the same time are: you have to be willing to help the person without concern that the person might take advantage of you, and the person has to go in not hoping to take advantage of you. These two conditions cannot be tested. In other words, if you see someone who is down, and you stretch out your hand to lift the person up, you cannot do this only hoping to spend just enough effort that it takes to get the person on his feet. You will have trouble determining just how long to allow the person to hold on before you decide to let go. It will be up to you to help a person and up to the person to also want to stand on his own two feet while you help him.

So, a person whose mindset is to want to help people but who at the same time does not want people to take advantage of him will be met with the same outcome or condition as a person who is looking for the answer to how to become more intelligent. The reason is that they are both looking for a line of demarcation; a line that does not exist. The same is true for the associate at the hotel because of the nobody-ever-told-me-that attitude. The associate is essentially saying that management will never be off the hook until it has shown and trained the associate on everything that could possibly come up that is related to the associate's job responsibilities. This person was looking for a line, one that does not exist. This associate was looking for excuses, and this is not a mindset for anyone whose intentions are to acquire knowledge, to learn.

A person who wants to know how we become more intelligent, or who essentially wants to know at what point he can consider himself intelligent, is like a person who tries to test his fiancé before he gets married to her. His options or outcomes, either way, will have changed. If his fiancé fails the test, he will disappointingly call off the relationship – he tested her for that reason. If the fiancé passes the test, and they move forward with their lives together but she later finds out that her trust was tested – which she will – the possibilities on how she looks at him will have changed forever. A man who tests his wife has the same mindset as the man who wants to know when to call himself intelligent in that they are both looking for a moment, a line that they can cross. It is not the end of the world to go about things this way. Remember, though, that our conversation is about what is possible – not what is right or what is wrong, just what is possible.

It is in the same line of thinking that I have considered that a person has no reason to think that he is good at what he does. This is not any different from saying that a person has no reason to think that he is intelligent. My position is that a person has no reason to think that he is good at what he does for two reasons. The first reason is that a person coexists with other people, so he is fundamentally only as good as the people with whom he coexists. The other reason is that a person can use the time he intends to spend assessing how good he is on other things he does not already know and on training the people with whom he coexists (this derives from the first point).

What we know is that I could have written a book that goes like this:

So we were all ready to head out to the party. I looked at myself in the mirror and thought, "Wow. I look good." My two buddies weren't too shabby either. Anyway, we got downstairs and the limousine was not there. One of my buddies looked at me and said, "Dude, what is going on? We cannot be late to this party. It would literally be the end of the world if we were late to this party." I placed a call and found out that the limousine we rented had mechanical problems and a backup was on the way. Well, the backup limousine left little to desire and my friend's girlfriend, in her words, "Would rather be caught dead in a yugo…"

It would have been just fine if I had written a book about hanging out with my friends. However, I decided to write a book that had a perspective on hanging out with my friends or being in a relationship or working with people, and so on. And it is in the effort that it takes to write such a book that I saw ideas as being equivalent to dumbbells of different weights. For instance, the idea that guns should be allowed in schools is like a dumbbell of a certain weight, and the idea that guns should not be allowed in schools also has a weight. Abortion should be legal is an idea of a certain weight. Abortion should be outlawed is an idea of a certain weight. Women should not be allowed to wear pants is an idea of a certain weight, and so is women should not be allowed to drive. Cell phones are necessary to have is an idea. An employer who does not allow associates to use Facebook at work will soon be extinct is an idea. Right handed people are smarter than left-handed people is an idea – it has a weight. There are all sorts of ideas that we ponder every day, and how we examine these ideas is like how a person within the community of weightlifters interacts with dumbbells.

Depending on the weight of a dumbbell, a person might not be able to lift it at all. Some might pick it up and immediately ram it into the mirror walls at the gym causing all kinds of havoc. Some might be able to drag it from one spot to another. Some people might only be able to lift a dumbbell just once because it is too heavy for them. Some people might be able to lift the dumbbell for different ranges of multiple repetitions and even keep good form while doing it. In this light, we can expect that if there is a community where the order of the day is weight lifting, then their weights, their dumbbells, would be equivalent to what ideas represent for the human society. That is, the variety of ways that the community can use the various dumbbells represents different outcomes or conditions. In the same way, the various ways in which we are able to look at and use ideas, the driver for the human society, determines our outcomes. As it would not be a right or wrong condition if no one in the community of weightlifters ever touched a dumbbell, so would it not be a crime if we were unable to exercise an idea thoroughly with our minds. It would not be the end of the world, only we would not know what is possible.

I realized in my analogy that I could consider that the body is to the community of weightlifters what the mind is to the human community. If we landed in the community or planet of weightlifters, here are some possibilities we might encounter. One possibility is that we might notice that the people do not spend time interacting with their dumbbells at all – flabby bodies might be commonplace. We might witness a scenario in which a little girl is stock under a car, and three or four people could not quickly dash to the car and lift it to free the little girl, or they might not be able to lift it without panting heavily and having one or two of them pass out from not being physically fit enough for the exercise that helping lift up a car is. Another possibility is that we could see a lot of fit and conditioned people. We could even see more extremely fit and conditioned people, indicating to us heavier dumbbells are being manufactured and used within the community. We could see a community where people are able to get to trapped little girls quicker; and one where lifting vehicles becomes less of an effort. We could see a community where people are able to generate more energy if it turned out that they also used their fitness to generate power for the community.

As human beings, our option is to ponder ideas. As I have said earlier, this job should be central to the way we see ourselves because it determines our outcomes. We do not have to do it. We do not have to ponder ideas, but it is an option that we have. If we find ourselves to have come across a particular idea, we would find ourselves dissecting the idea with great ease and coming to a useful conclusion on its utility for society, and vice versa. For instance, if we find ourselves moving items between two rooms that are adjoined by a door, we might come up with the idea of keeping the door open for ease of passage between both rooms. We may decide to use one of the human movers to hold the door open, while the remaining movers do the work. We may devise a different way to keep the door open, thinking that we value the additional help of the person who would otherwise be holding the door open. We could end up spending all day figuring out how to do this – keeping the door open and not using a person to do it – if, for instance, we had not had to do it before. In any case, the outcome would not be the end of the world, but it is our mind and its capacity that would determine this outcome that we would end up living with.

Imagine what any of us could do with any given idea of the day. Would we take the idea and completely turn it on its head because our mind could not handle it? This would be equivalent to what would happen to a person whose physical conditioning was not at the level of the dumbbell he tried to lift, and chaos ensued.

At this juncture, I should raise an important observation. My observation is that in the human society, we have this thing where we elect leaders. My observation about this is that when we elect leaders, we seem to be saying, "We realize that we all live together, and that requires some coordination." We seem to be saying that there are tons of ideas that we will float from time to time, as individuals, as groups of people, as local communities, and we should have a town hall and a moderator, or moderators at various levels, to help bring and keep those ideas in the forefront. I see a need for organization, one necessitated by the condition that is a bunch of people coexisting.

I have thought that it is fascinating that we elect leaders. I have also thought that the kind of leaders we elect – which in itself is a condition – leads to all sorts of outcomes, all sorts of possibilities. As a result, I have thought that if there was a society where what people did was play tennis, it would matter in terms of outcome, if the leader they elected was Andre Agassi, or if it was someone who had never seen a tennis racket before. It would cause a change in the daily life of a community that talked about and played tennis if the leader they chose played some tennis, played high level tennis, knew about playing on different surfaces, is technically sound when it came to serving, or if he had never played tennis before.

I take our condition, the one in which we have resorted to electing leaders, very seriously because of the outcomes that it can create. For instance, a leader may decide that in order to settle disagreement, his most useful option will be to kill those who disagree with him. Of course, an outcome like this still would not be the end of the world. If a leader, for whatever reason, thinks that 'western' education is bad for the world and as a result pursues policies that he considers to be in opposition to western values, the outcome that this would create for his society would not be the end of the world. If the leader in our tennis community thought it also counted when the ball went long, it would not be the end of the world.

However, if there is any point to make in the thought that the mind is what to accelerate, as I said earlier, it would be worth thinking that a leader of a certain orientation could play a role in that acceleration. In other words, if two people were playing tennis for the leadership position in a community where what people did was play tennis, it would matter to the community which of the two candidates became the leader. Five years later, we could compare outcomes for that community in terms of where they all end up in their skill level if the professional became the leader instead of the individual who had never seen a tennis racket. The difference in outcome might include whether the community found a passion for the game and how that would change the conversation about the sport of tennis. The outcome that could be created when the elected leader is a passionate player might include a national program that inspired young citizens for love of the game, for instance.

Since I see the world in a light similar to one where a man applies a door stop to the back of the door, since we live in a world where leaders are elected to represent their people, since our minds and the way we use it is the determinant for our outcomes, it helps to wonder with what 'weights' we, and the leaders who are elected, exercise our minds. It helps to examine our orientation.

My point is this: Saying that a person's job is to think is like saying that a person's job is to avoid defects. A defect is anything that is contrary to what is to be demonstrated, to what will prevail, to what will become evident. Essentially, a person has to be able to think precisely the appropriate thought to avoid a defect. This is no easy task because the ability to think the appropriate thought is achieved only when a person has made provisions to improve his logic – his ability to think a valid thought.

For things to work out for the man who wants to keep a door open so that he does not create a defect (that which prevails in his situation), for things to work out between the diner and the waitress, for things to work out between two lovebirds trying to figure out how to advance their relationship, for things to work out without a defect in the community where lifting weights comes in handy for when little girls get stuck under heavy objects, for things to work out without defects in a world where we all coexists, we have to imagine that we have gotten to the place where we think the appropriate thought in every situation. We have to be assured that we have the appropriate framework for how we manufacture the thoughts that we use to create outcomes, the thoughts that we use to make the world look the way it does.

So, a thought has to have an element of a useful starting point(for that which is to be demonstrated), it has to allow for improvement or testing or unceasing dialogue, and its outcome has to orient us to what is possible.

In our coexistence, here is a thought appropriate for politics. In his inaugural address of 2008, President Barack Obama said this:

"The question we ask today is not whether our government is too big or too small, but whether it works[2] –"

I thought that this was a particularly relevant thing to say because in a country where one side is traditionally identified as big-government advocates and the other side is deemed a small government advocate, what was missing was a Useful Starting Point thought. The useful starting point here as articulated by Mr. Obama is it is not whether something is big or small; it is whether it works. It is whether government works. That is, it is possible for government to be big and not work, and it is possible for government to be small and not work.

Since what the human society is employed to do is to think, to use our minds, to ponder ideas and use those ideas to manipulate our outcomes, the thought of electing a leader who is good at thinking the same way that someone may be good at playing tennis or lifting weights, is also a useful starting point. It would be like saying that we have realized that if thinking is what we did, it should be institutionalized. It should be the order of the day. This of course is better facilitated by electing people who are good at it. In other words, if you lived in a community of tennis players, and the leader of the community is an excellent tennis player who plays tennis every day and talks about tennis every time you see him on television whereby he even throws in pointers for beginners, and he has a weekly show, this would have a certain outcome on your personal passion for the game different than if the leader had never seen a racket and could not care less for the game.

The statement included in Mr. Obama's inaugural speech is a change in the game. It is similar to what would happen to a community of people who have only been ankle-deep in water if one day someone who has been waist-deep in water shows up. If for ten, fifty, or a hundred years, the people in this community had only been ankle deep every time they went to the river, they could only have developed a knowledge base consistent with that of a person who has only been ankle-deep in water. Now, if one day a person shows up, one or two of them anyway, who may have ventured in waist deep and begins to question the collective conversation, two things will happen. The first thing that will happen is that there will be tension, or intensity, because someone is now saying new or different things, and people will be forced to reconsider their positions. The second thing that will happen is that there will be divergence. That is, ideas that were spawned by people who have been in water ankle deep that seemed moderately sound will begin to look far less sound once the community begins to ponder the river from the experience of waist immersion.

One morning, years ago, I walked into the breakfast room at the hotel and found three of my staff members sitting and having a quick bite. I made it clear to them that it was inappropriate, and they immediately packed up and left. In the ensuing conversation, they told me that the reason they went in the breakfast room, which had never happened before, was because the employee break room had been torn down for what was a small face lift. It immediately occurred to me that though this had never happened before, it did not mean that my staff knew to not sit and have breakfast in the dining room alongside guests. It did not mean that they had a body of knowledge that they could have used to choose otherwise. The reason I had never found my staff in the breakfast room and having breakfast perhaps alongside hotel guest is not because they held certain standards that would consider the act inappropriately and unprofessional. Rather, it had not happened only because they had not been tested. The break room renovation was an event that tested what my staff thought they knew about their relationship with our guests and how it impacted our operational goals. If the break room had not become unavailable, I would have continued to assume that my staff had a level of awareness about how we all conducted ourselves in the breakfast room during breakfast hours.

The presidency of Barack Obama is to history what the staff break room renovation was to our hotel operation. The presidency of Barack Obama has caused things to happen that otherwise would not have happened had someone else become president, including things that could accelerate our minds regarding the ideas that we currently talk about, and new ideas that our minds can become capable of creating. I would like to think that I have become more engaged in thinking in very recent years as a result of not only what is happening in my personal life, but also how the social dialogue has changed. Ultimately, the possibilities that are being created by this event, by the presidency of Barack Obama, are capable of changing our condition, specifically by accelerating the mind.

1

WHEN A BAD THING HAPPENS, A BAD THING HAS HAPPENED

In a world where we all live together, where we coexist, what are the possibilities? How do we do it? Where could we find the framework for how to go about life?

The 'you lie[3]' outburst by Representative Joe Wilson during President Barack Obama's health care speech in September 2009 was something Roland Martin of CNN could have used two years later in his article titled: 'Obama's problem? No one fears him.'

When I saw this headline by Mr. Martin, one thought immediately came to my mind. I did, however, want to read the article first. By the time I was finished reading the article, I had two thoughts to chew on. My first thought was that every leader is really only one incitement away from turning into a tyrant. I am confident that there are leaders, managers, community leaders, presidents of nations, who may have made decisions not because those decisions were useful, but rather for completely different reasons. I realize that the expectation of most in the world today is to try to make decisions that portray them as 'strong.' We see the outcomes of such a mindset all around us. According to Roland Martin, "It is abundantly clear that President Obama is unwilling to fire back at his critics, who disrespect him and the office of the president. He wants to take the high ground, while his critics are ripping the ground out from underneath him. Instead of taking charge of his agenda, he is willing to let others blow him off to pursue their own.[4]"

We all, including Mr. Martin, should concede that a world where a person lives to fire back at his critics, one where he wants to ensure that people 'fear' him, has its outcome. It is really only a condition. And if this is only one outcome, why should we limit ourselves to it? What is to say that there are no other outcomes, other conditions? Can we expect that a person may have thought that he could generate other different outcomes when his driver is not to invoke fear in the people he governs? If a leader has had it with people yelling at him during his speeches, with concessions that he thinks he has made time and again with his opposition, with supporters suggesting he needs a stronger backbone, he will, in fact, find himself in a completely different possibility as he attempts to compensate.

The second thing that I thought when I read Mr. Martin's article is more omni-cognitive in terms of what works, what prevails, what is possible in our cohabiting reality.

When a bad thing happens, a bad thing has happened.

If there is a person who has decided that what he is going to do is throw a wrench in your work, you will have two non-negotiable burdens. The first burden is the one in which you find a way to create something that works, however long that takes. The person whose intentions are to disrupt it does not have this burden. The second burden that you have is that of convincing the person not to throw a wrench in your work. This also is an only option. The reason for this being an only option is that if the person goes ahead and throws a wrench in your work, there is actually really not a whole lot you can do. Your condition becomes even more challenging if the person is, in fact, convinced that throwing a wrench in your work is the right thing for him to do.

Does a person who is convicted of a crime he has not committed, one for which he serves time, go for vengeance upon vindication? Or does he say to himself, "What sort of outcome am I prepared to create?"

If you are a society of people who have been oppressed for decades, and you fight every day for your freedom in the face of unspeakable evil and oppression, and one day it finally happens, and you gain your freedom, you will have possibilities with regards to the sort of society your collective mind can form to cohabit with those who used to be your oppressors. Would you hope to create a society that seeks retribution and violence against those who wronged you? Would you pursue this as a possibility? Would you consume yourself in an exercise of reconciliation and forgiveness? We live in a world where we create outcomes every single day and in every situation that arises. In this one very condition, this one very outcome, where it is done, you have been wronged, or your society has endured years of suffering and inequality[5], how have you weighed what sort of outcome to make of it?

I have not said this in a simple manner of choosing alternatives. I have only implied this as ideas equivalent to weights for the mind to exercise. I have said this to imply that if ideas were equal to dumbbells of various weights, would we care to exercise them? Whether a person decides to exercise the dumbbells or not is fine; it will not mean the end of the world. It will, however, make it clear to us all that ideas, like dumbbells, are out there, and whether we are able to exercise them or not determines what the world looks like.

There is a world, for instance, commensurate with the idea: **You cannot war yourself to peace. You cannot anger yourself into friendship with another.** Of course, if that idea weighs 200 pounds but the strongest of any of us can only lift 170 pounds, such is a world we would not be able to realize, not until we work our way up to that strength level, anyway.

What option does the person who knows have in making others see what he sees? If you live in a village where peoples' experience revolve around the village river and everyone has only been ankle-deep in the water and the village conversations reflected it, you as the only person who has been waist-deep in water will have a burden. Your burden is that you know. Your burden also is that you have to make others see what you see. Should you yell at them? Should you insult them every waking moment? Should you be angry at them?

It would not be the end of the world if no one comes along with you on a journey. For you and for the rest of the village, it is about what is possible, what outcomes you are able to create.

If you are walking down the street, and you run into someone whose shirt you like, there is one of three ways by which the shirt could come into your possession. The first way the shirt could become yours is if you round up your friends, beat the living day light out of the shirt guy, and take his shirt. Of course, with this outcome that you are creating, you have to wonder if you are the kind of person who likes to sleep with his eyes open. And the person whose shirt you took also has to decide if he wants to spend the rest of his life making sure that you do not get away with it.

The second way you could get to own the shirt is by turning into a con man. You could sweet-talk the guy, gaining his confidence. He would not see it coming. But then again, you would have to wonder how long before he figures out that he was being duped. The third way is that you could introduce yourself to the stranger, let him know you like his shirt as you get to know him, and let him willingly give you his shirt because you also have things you can offer him.

We are limited by the outcomes that we create. If a person sees a world where he is convinced that the way to get what he wants is by being ruthless, we should acknowledge that this is really only an option. It is not a right or wrong thing. It is not the end of the world. It is, however, about what is possible.

One day, I got to my hotel and found my staff in the middle of a conversation. Something did not get done because one or two people decided that it was not their job. It actually got done; somebody went ahead and did it. Now, when I called a meeting about this event, it was obvious that what some were expecting, certainly what the person who ended up doing the job was expecting was that I would come down hard on the people who said it was not their job.

The conversation I wanted to have, however, was not about how I was going to punish anyone who did not do his or her job. When a bad thing happens, a bad thing has happened. The conversation that I wanted to have with my staff was one that would reassure me that I was not working with a bunch of people who spent their days sorting out which part of what they did was their job and which part was not. There is a hotel whose reality is commensurate to that.

It did not surprise me that there were some who had trouble with me, some who were more focused on what I was going to do to those who abandoned their responsibility. For some of these associates, it even took me a while to convince them not to focus on the person who had an it-is-not-my-job way of looking at things. It took me a while to convince some that if a person says it is not my job, step in with an it-is-okay-I-will-do-it attitude.

What I am going to do to the person who sees a workplace in a this-is-my-job-that-one-is-not light is the least of my concerns. It pales. I am trying to create possibilities for what we are able to accomplish as a business. This is my Useful Starting Point for what is possible for us.

2

THE CONFLICTS OF THE MIND ARE NOT WHOLLY MULTIFACETED

There are two conditions, one to the right and the other to the left. There are only two types of people in the world. There are people who want things to work out, and there are people who do not want things to work out. There are people who put others first, and there are people who put themselves first. There are people who want to be in a relationship, and there are people who do not want to be in a relationship. There are people who are convinced in a situation that they are right, and there are people who know that there is a chance that they could be wrong. There are those who think that perception is reality or that perception is part of reality, and there are those who think that perception is not reality or that only reality is reality. There are those who think that we are all in this together, and there are those who think that we are in this individually and for ourselves. These are all ideas in what is possible. In a world where we live in one outcome or another, to say that the conflicts of the mind are not wholly multi-faceted, in itself, is a position that has its own outcome.

When a person approaches your door, there is really only one of two things you could say. One of the things you could say is, "come on in," and the other one is, "go away." Trying to sort out the conflicts in the mind is work. It is really hard work. It is as difficult as going through what it takes to go to the gym and work out, and over time look very fit and conditioned. What is clear is that there are not too many options for resolving the conflicts that tear at us inside. Unfortunately, it does not appear that we have even made the commitment to pursue a resolution for this important change that is the key to what sort of society and future we continue to fashion. Just like a person who wants to be strong and fit has to start by concluding that he has to commit to working out, we have to commit to the connection between wanting to advance our minds and what that means for society. This is a matter of a useful starting point.

If a person decides to leave Orlando, Florida for Valdosta, Georgia, doubtless there is a lot that he should keep in mind, but none of which may have bearing for his useful starting point. The useful starting point is not what time of the day it is. It is not what car he is driving or if he is fueled up. It is not how he is dressed or whether he is wearing his glasses. The useful starting point for a man who wants to get to Valdosta from Orlando is that he is heading north.

By the time I heard Mitt Romney say, "I like being able to fire people who provide services to me," my thoughts were already rapidly changing, or rather forming, around a particular strain of outcome that I thought was compelling me as a manager to look at firing people less so as something to like. Certainly, when I was a much younger manager, I liked to fire people because I thought it meant that I was a no-nonsense manager, a proactive go getter who was not afraid to use his authority. Now, I do not look at people in a sink or swim sort of way anymore. I look at people in a swim sort of way. It is this investment that would make it difficult for me, on the day that I have to let a person go, to bring myself to say, "I enjoy firing that person."

There is one other reason why I am in my condition. The person that I fire is still my problem. The person that I fire will take his 'sorry' self and find a job with another business that I can guarantee will do business with me either directly or indirectly. So where is my I-like-to-be-able-to-fire-people pride?

I took my car for a wash one day at a local business that I frequented. When I pulled up, I expressed to the attendant that I had recently had my clutch repaired, and that I needed to be sure that whoever would drive my car through the car wash could drive a manual transmission car. My reason for asking the question was not because I had my clutch repaired but because on multiple occasions after a car wash, I had noticed a strong burned clutch smell. In fact, on one of the occasions, the attendant who drove my car through the wash had commented that he had trouble driving it. At this point, the valet attendant had no choice but to ask the driver about to take my car through the wash if he could drive manual transmission, who admitted that he did not know how to drive it.

Inside, I engaged the cashier, who appeared to be wife and co-owner, on a different level. I told her my story noting that while I was not necessarily making a correlation between my visits to the car wash and having had to repair my clutch, in light of the times that I had experienced burned clutch smells and a driver admitting to having had trouble driving my car and the close call where someone who did not know how to drive a manual transmission was about to jump in my car, as a business owner myself, I was interested in their hiring practices, and if it included at the minimum hiring drivers who could drive both automatic and manual transmission vehicles. My intentions were to have a conversation with another business operator about the challenges and successes and the passion it takes to get from good to great.

The lady, perhaps for unfounded fear of any liabilities, was quick to reject my claim. She simply made it clear to me that she had been operating her car wash for eight years without any such complaints and that what I should have done was stayed in my car and drove it through the car wash myself. She also made it clear to me that the receptionist with whom I spoke outside, the one who presented herself as a manager and was ready to take charge and help, was not a manager and that if I did not like their services, I should take my car elsewhere.

I found the owner's response shocking and disappointing as a customer. The first thing I thought was that she did not need to tell me that the receptionist was not a manager. The most basic service orientation helps articulate that it is really of no use to the customer what title a person holds but rather whether that person can take charge of a situation at hand, which the receptionist appeared to be doing. Further, how disappointing and discouraging it has to be for the poor receptionist to find that her employer does not care to empower her to take ownership of customer service situations.

The second thing I thought was how odd it was that the co-owner thought that her having been in business for eight years automatically proved her expertise in the car wash business. I literally chuckled at this thought that just because she had had no complaints implied that she was good at what she did. I really thought that she was going to say that she had been in business for, say, more than twenty-five years. In most business environments, eight years is not enough time to develop a sophisticated operation, to demonstrate competence. It is no defense at all. Also, the fact that she had had no such complaint as mine might just mean that her customers may not have thought to connect their clutch repairs and their trips to the car wash. Of course, her defense to take my business elsewhere or drive my car through the car wash myself was my personal ode to capitalism.

This story of my experience at the car wash is a bit of a digression. I have certainly said more than I needed to for the point I am attempting to make. However, it was my story at the time, back in 2010, and I have presented it here practically the same way I wrote it then. At the time, I was disappointed and angry and critical of this car wash establishment, one business operator to another. I thought that the business lacked care and passion, and that it deserved to be punished. I wanted to create a business index that would help us find and punish, by not patronizing, businesses such as this car wash, and instead patronize with intention those for whom running their business is a labor of love. I thought that society simply would be better off.

Fast forward two years, and I started to feel differently about the idea in substantial and substantive ways.

There are two types of people in the world. There are people who are quick to say 'damn you,' and there are people who are convinced that their destiny is eternally connected to those of others. I was having a conversation with someone during the time when the health care debate was at the center of the national consciousness. My acquaintance had a cut-no-one-no-slack - let them die - you cannot use my money - take some responsibility, view of the discussion. This was a condition, an outcome. This was fine. It was not going to be the end of the world. I, on the other hand, had started to think, at the time, and this was my example, that even though I did not have kids because I concluded that I could not afford them, I acknowledged that the person who had five or six with sixth or seventh on the way was my problem. I had not arrived at such a condition because I was a sympathetic person, not at all. In fact, I made the point that if there was a way to have people whom anyone in any respect deemed was 'burdening' society to live on a different planet, then the 'let's punish them attitude' would work. However, as long as we all live together, their burden would cross mine.

I thought that I contributed more when I did not ditch this car wash but continued to engage them in ways that improved their operations.

3

WE SHOULD HAVE CALLED A MEETING

We should have had a meeting to make arrangements, to find out how plain and clear things are.

A useful starting point would be for us to know that as a species what we have in common is that we live on the planet earth. I do not think that we started out by having that meeting or that we have had that meeting.

Every day at my business, I make sure that people know that we are a hotel. Most people, rudimentarily, are not aware of the significance of this mindset, but because it is the basis for our training, they inescapably deal with the process, some people, in ways that help us refine it. Every day, I have a meeting with myself and my staff to check what we know, to make sure that we are indeed running a hotel as opposed to, say, a gas station. Though it often seems like a joke to my staff when I go through this process, it is an important starting point for me. They often find it to be an important exercise too when their knowledge of our condition, or environment, is tested. An example of our demonstration of the awareness of what sort of a business we are in is the fact that my housekeeping department comes to work in the morning hours and cleans and prepares all of our rooms for new occupancy because our check out time is noon and a person who reserves a room can expect that room to be ready no later than 3:00 p.m.

On any given day when we find that a guest has not departed from our room by noon, we would consult with him. We would essentially let him know that he is at a point where he has to decide because we are at a point where we have to decide. In fact, there was a day when a guest apparently yelled "go away" at a room attendant. The staff member brought this to my attention and needed to know what to do. The staff member was concerned that going back would upset the guest even more. This was one way to see the situation. What I told my staff member was that we would go back and explain to our guest why we were knocking on his door. So, we went up and explained to this guest our commitments to him and to a bunch of other people who would be calling our hotel home that evening. The guest was not upset at all. He realized that we knew what we were doing, and he helped us facilitate our operation immediately. We had a meeting with him. He knew immediately that he had to decide to leave, or to extend his stay.

Every day at the hotel, we have a meeting. It is of absolutely no surprise to me that my housekeeping department has not, perhaps in revolt, decided that they would come to clean rooms at midnight and not at 9:00 in the morning. I find this to be a useful starting point for our operation. We have a meeting. We tell ourselves that we are a hotel and not a race course, or an airline company, or magicians on a road show, or a gas station.

Recently, my girlfriend called to tell me that she had a great idea. Her idea was that we should not see each other for a month. Now, I sort of knew why she would come up with something like that in the first place. She had talked about stepping up her work out at the gym, not that she needed it. I figured she wanted to be sure that any results from her fitness escapade would be more so noticeable if I had not seen her for a while. That was what I was thinking. Not that it really mattered, because, a little over a week later, one of her friends flew into town, and we all decided to go out for dinner. This is where I got into trouble because apparently when I met up with them, my sweet girlfriend thought that I did not show, that it did not show, that I had not seen her in over a week. Okay, may be this is the part where every woman in the world starts to lecture me on just what I did wrong, and the part where every man in the world advises me on the futility of psychoanalyzing a woman. Either way, the event had a my-girlfriend-and-I-need-to-have-a-meeting written all over it.

I first started to wonder about the basis for the reaction that my girlfriend was hoping to elicit from me. What sort of response had she assumed I would offer after having gone a week without seeing each other. This contemplation prodded me, in a broader context, to want to draw similarities in my girlfriend's constitution, or basis, and that which has led us to say things like, "absence makes the heart grow fonder," or led us to think that "perception is reality," or conclude that "familiarity breeds contempt," or assume that "guns don't kill people - people kill people," or wonder if "survival of the fittest" makes any more sense than thinking that there is an association between facial structures and crime. Further, I realized that I was not looking for answers to these specific questions, the same way that I am not necessarily interested in unraveling my girlfriend. I thought that if the reason we say these things is because we have heard them so many times, or that we have grown accustomed to saying them, in contrast to the notion that these things really make sense, and that we actually know the sense that they make, then I should pursue a different approach to finding answers than trying to unravel individually phrases that we have managed to throw together over time.

I needed to have a meeting with my girlfriend for the same reasons we need to have a meeting as people. **My point is, we are here, wherever this is, doing whatever it is that human beings do, but I** am not sure if we started out by calling a meeting to say, "Folks, we are here, and if there is some sense that this place makes, let's get out there and try to find what that is, and figure this thing out, that way we do not go throwing words together just because we can, or thinking things just because we are able to. And, if things do not make sense, as in, if we are not supposed to be poking around trying to find how one thing connects to another, in this place where we have found ourselves, then it is all wide open, let's have some fun doing whatever it is our little hearts desire, without one person telling the other what to do or how to act." I doubt that we started with this sort of understanding, this sort of arrangement, these ground rules, this orientation.

Essentially, I figured that the meeting I wanted to have with my girlfriend needed not to be about how to react after I had not seen her for a week, the same way that the meeting we ought to have could not just be to answer the question, "is perception reality?" or the question, "does familiarity breed contempt?" How many of these type questions am I going to have to address with my girlfriend? And how many are we going to have to answer as a community of human beings? The analogy that I thought of as I try to find a way to approach my two similar challenge – my coexisting with my girlfriend, and human coexistence – is this: I would like to jump off a cliff right now, but before I do, I would like to know if that is something I could do freely, whereby I am able to fulfill personal desires about what happens after I jump off a cliff. I thought that if what happens after I jump off a cliff is not entirely up to me, I have more serious things to figure out first that would address more than my desires for what I would want the outcome of jumping off a cliff to be.

This observation compelled me to think further that there is something else that may supersede whether there is sense that I need to uncover or not. I thought I could acknowledge that if there were sense, that just meant that there are rules that we should uncover, and to which we should conform, or that we should acknowledge and apply.

If, however, there were no sense, in this place where we all live together, we could not get by without some ground rules either. So, I found myself thinking that whether there is preexisting sense or not, the only way we could make anything work is by having, or making up, sense, anyway. It gets better. It gets better because it seems that we would not need to second guess ourselves about whether the ground rules we set are made up or preexisting rules that we have to find and with which we have to comply for one very simple 'litmus' test. All we have to do is find out if it works or not. If we took things seriously enough, I thought that this was where we would start. This made calling a meeting all the more important. This made defining our 'sense' or finding sense, one and the same. This makes being guided by the thought, "does it work," a fundamental preoccupation.

In "making up" sense or uncovering what sense preexists, in figuring out in what context should I have a meeting with my girlfriend, what treatment to give to how we react to each other based on time apart, or her physical fitness goals; in determining what approach guides a bunch of human beings living together, I thought we could use a hotel as an example. We could start by establishing that a hotel is not the same as a gas station. This would be a useful starting point. The place where I go when I need to lay my head down and get some sleep is not the same place where I take my vehicle when it runs out of gas. I have had a brush with the seriousness of what is metaphysical – what is real, what is true whether we come into contact with it or not - once before when I was in college. My soccer coach left me a message in recruitment efforts for the upcoming season saying, "if there is what is, where is it?" This was in response to my outgoing telephone message where I proclaimed with youthful zest, "if there is what is, then there is what is." Yes, there is so much that we could make of that comment, and we will get to it, fundamentally.

For now, there is a reason we are able to distinguish between what is a hotel and what is a gas station, even if it is reason that we made up. If, however, we begin to doubt ourselves, or if we should be afraid that we may not know what we think we know, or if what we are searching for is validation, or if what we want to know is if this is permanent enough, in an epistemological sort of way, or if I have to wonder how I acquire knowledge, all I have to do the next time someone comes into my hotel to rent a room is to offer him gasoline for his vehicle and see how that goes over. How do we know what we think we know? Is it through our senses? Or is it by some divine intervention? Let us not get fanciful. Let us just say, if we decide that a hotel is not the same as a truck stop, there are no more questions to answer. Seriously.

If I can build a hotel, then maybe I am past the point of wondering if I am dreaming or not, and maybe there is an infrastructure that allows me to do that. In any case, here I am with a hotel that I have to run, and I am wondering, how should I run it? I realize here that I am essentially running a business, and my objective is to make the business profitable. One of the ways I could facilitate profitability is not to spend so much money washing the bed sheets every time that I rent a room. Is this something I should do? Or will it cause me to lose sleep at night? Will the people to whom I rent rooms think it is okay? Or will they think that it is unethical? Whose idea is it that we wash those sheets after each guest, and clean up the rooms? Who came up with such standards? Are we doing this because it is the right thing to do?

And that is not all. With a hotel on my hands, I have hired people to help me operate it. I have concluded that I am not dreaming. Well, it actually does not matter anymore at this point if I am dreaming or not. I have a hotel to run, and I need a bunch of people to help me run it. I have to establish who does what, and how we should act toward one another so that we could make things work. The way we reason and interact has to align with accomplishing hotel goals that we have set. It would be hilarious if the politics of the front-desk department do not dovetail with that of the housekeeping department. With a check out time of noon and a check in time of 3 pm and beyond, if the housekeeping department decides that they would prefer to work at midnight, this would cause damning problems with regards to the renting of clean rooms. Things can get complicated pretty fast, or they can get pretty simple, depending on how we decide to work together.

Finally, there is a race we are running as a hotel operation. There is a light toward which we are turning, a perfection for which we strive. One day, in an attempt to explain the aesthetics of what we do as a hotel to an associate, I made the point that in operating our business, our goal is not to be nice to people, unlike how one might rudimentarily think that perception is the same as reality. In pure, tested fashion, though it may come across that way, the same way that a person might come across as beautiful or a painting might be visually appealing, what we are doing is not trying to be nice to people; the beauty that we work at perfecting is that of delivering the best service and the best product that we can provide to our guests. These two things are not the same. Being nice to people and providing people with service, which can be construed as being nice, are different things. Inevitably, this will become evident. There is a dimension to what we do that transcends what is seen physically. We know this. We know that there is something that we can give a person, a guest, that is objective rather than subjective, something that is more permanent than how attractive the associate at the desk is or the thread count in our linen, because that is not the beauty that sets us apart from the other hotels, that is not the purity that obtains.

I have taken notice that Barack Obama has traveled across the world giving speeches that are loaded with ideas, or weights, that can create so many possibilities, so many outcomes. Though he gets mocked for it, I get the sense that all he is trying to say is, "We really should have a meeting and define a few things, agree on a few things."

If one day you walk into a room and you find a group of people with an aisle between them, and you find them pointing fingers at each other on who is to blame for things that are not getting done, and the one side says, "you have to come up with serious solutions," as the other side says the same thing, I hope you would not think that the reason these factions have found themselves in the situation they are in is that they know what they are doing. I hope you would not think that the reason they are acting the way they are is that they are far more intelligent than the situation that they have to fix. Also, it is actually not their fault, it is not a fault that they have found themselves in this condition. However, it would be worth contemplating if they might be able to say that the only way for them to get out of the situation that they are in is to become more intelligent than they are at that point. A useful starting point for this is the admission that the only reason we are acting this way right now is that it is the best way our minds would allow us to act. However, if we improve our minds, we would see that we could act differently.

With myself, I must call a meeting. If I heard that somebody said that somebody said that my mother is the devil, have I thought about what is the way to react to this, what conditions or outcomes I would want to create for myself and for the world afterwards? In one of his speeches to the United Nations Assembly, President Barack Obama pretty much said this, "Let us decide how we want to react when we get upset for whatever reason. It is about what outcome we want to create. For me, I am thinking that burning down a restaurant does not fill an empty stomach. So, I am thinking that this is probably not a useful starting point. Neither is people who take all the country's resources for themselves.[6]"

4

IT IS OKAY TO BE 'WEAK'

I am more curious of the likelihood that if pressed, we would find that we may not even know what we mean when we describe a person as weak. We may not succeed in making the point that a person is weak.

One day, I was having a telephone conversation with my boss. He had asked me a question to which I did not know the answer. Instead of telling him the truth, I went on a rant. I went on for a good minute, and he was just quiet. After some time, he said to me, "Christian, you could just say that you don't know."

This book is about the outcomes, the possibilities that we are able to create. And it presupposes that an outcome is guaranteed, regardless of whether we have paid attention or not. I have already concluded that things will happen, whether we are incredibly knowledgeable or not, whether we have done our homework or not. Either way, it is not the end of the world. It would not be the end of the world if we were not pondering this right now, if you were not reading this book, or if we were not examining what sort of outcomes we create. So, it would not be the end of the world if a person lives his life never wanting to appear weak – or appear to be whatever it is that we have defined as weak.

A whole nation may have gone to war because the leader needed to appear decisive. He had to appear strong.

Remember that I have written this book to make the point that the reason we act the way we do is that we are not intelligent enough to act otherwise. I have made the point that this condition has nothing to do with who is smart and who is not or who is right and who is wrong. This is a waste of time for the mind. All there is to it is that we are surrounded by ideas, ideas that our minds can exercise based on how capable it is in order to create an outcome. This is just like how a person might go into the gym and attempt to lift a certain weight dumbbell. I have equated ideas with dumbbells. Some ideas weigh little, and some ideas are very heavy. A person might not be able to pick up a dumbbell of a certain weight. A person might pick up a dumbbell and start wobbling around and crash through the glass wall. A person might be able to do just one or two repetitions of exercise

with the dumbbell. A person might be able to do many repetitions with the dumbbell and not even show fatigue.

I was talking with friends some time back. We started off the conversation about whether guns killed people or people killed people. It was contentious. On why a person might need a gun in the first place, I referenced a person who might be of the position that if a person slapped you, it would be okay to turn the other cheek. We could imagine what choices a person would have if he walked up to the newspaper stand as he started the day, only to encounter a slap on the face from a total stranger. He would have to choose between two outcomes for what the rest of his day would look like. He could watch his day go down the proverbial drain, or he could diffuse the situation. Whatever a person in a situation like this decided to do would not be the end of the world. The options, of course, range from blowing everything up, to causing the perpetrator to go home, look at himself in the mirror and go, "what is wrong with me?" It would not be the end of the world if we thought that guns killed people. It would not be the end of the world if we thought that people killed people. It is all a game of outcomes, a game of what is possible.

I have thought about how to handle a person who decided not to pay his share of the utility bill. The idea of your roommate not paying you for his share of the apartment utility is equivalent to him backslapping your right cheek. If this happened, you could escalate the situation, lay one on him, and risk him saying, "now, I'm really not paying you." Your other option would be to turn the other cheek. You could make a case that would bring him to a place where he looked at himself in the mirror and said, "what is wrong with me?" If you were able to create this situation, albeit at a great expense, you might find it more useful, as would the next person who became the guy's roommate.

My interest is not whether a person turns the other cheek after getting slapped across the face. My interest is in the possibilities that we are able to create. I thought that it would be a matter of great interest, the possibilities or outcomes that we create, if our bases may have been manufactured. Using the roommate situation as an example, if it turned out that the reason two people escalated their differences was because one wanted to look bullish, and that the other, who may have been told one too many times that he was a push over, compensated and decided that things would be different that time; then the outcome would clearly be one based not on anything useful. There is an outcome created when the impetus for decisions made were that a person wanted not to look weak.

Some of the outcomes we continue to create could be traced to a person not wanting to appear weak. It might be why a person would describe the word compromise as when somebody agreed with his views.[7]

If we lived in a society where what we did was lift weights, an outcome we could create is one where a person who could barely lift a fifty-pound dumbbell regularly told a person who could lift one hundred-pound weights that the weights were the same. This would not constitute a useful starting point. It would not be the end of the world if a person could say such a thing without cost to him. If this person had said that a fifty-pound weight was as heavy as a hundred-pound weight often enough that he believed it, it would not be the end of the world. However, there is a world that is commensurate to that condition.

If everything we did was predicated on a person not wanting to say, "I do not know," we would have a world that reflected that. I have actually sat in business meetings where it was obvious to me that the reason a person kept pushing a point was not on its merit but rather because the person was bent on wanting his recommendation to be the one that was adopted. I have also heard people say that they did not like being wrong, or that they liked having their way.

The only struggle we are in is the one with our minds, each of us, individually, with no one else involved.

If you were driving down the left of a two lane interstate road, and as you came up on an on-ramp there was an eighteen wheeler coming on the ramp ready to merge, you would have a decision to make, especially if there was a small jeep in the right lane that would need to get over to make room for the rig. Given how all three vehicles were staggered, it would seem that you could let off the gas, thereby providing the jeep an option to change lanes if it simply could not power past the eighteen-wheeler. Of course, if you were the type of driver who did not like to let people in, or if you were the kind of person who did not like people getting in front of him, period, the situation could get dicey. If the driver of the jeep was the anxious kind who preferred back roads to multiple lanes and fast pace and rigs, this would not help the situation. And if the driver in the eighteen-wheeler had his own complex, well, he could really flex his muscle. If ultimately, no one let the eighteen-wheeler in, and he was forced to the shoulder, it could slow down traffic for him to get on.

A similar situation happened when I was getting on the on-ramp of a two lane interstate way. There were two or so cars in front of me and three or four cars behind me. As we were all speeding up to get into the busy traffic, the vehicles on the road were making room for us by changing to the left lane. As we were getting on, there was now room for the procession of cars, including mine, to leave the ramp lane in succession and enter the freed up right lane of the interstate. As I prepared to leave the ramp, I realized that the vehicle behind me had already merged and was speeding up to overtake me. In this order, by the time the vehicle was done overtaking me, the ramp lane that I was in would have run out, and I would be driving on the shoulder. So, I sped up and got in front of him just in time to have to slow down his momentum a bit. To no surprise, I could see the driver in my rear-view mirror expressing his frustrations. Of course, I hoped that he saw my expression asking him where he thought I was going to go. I am not taking this thought lightly at all. I have not thought that I was entitled to a turn or that the driver behind me should go out of his way to let me in. I remember that one day when I was in the check out lane at the grocery store, I could not keep letting people in front of me because that would prevent me from getting checked out, myself. It would be nice for the people to whom I extended a favor, but I had places to go too. At the end of the day, is it not about accomplishing one's goals? If a person who is ruthlessly ambitious joined the faculty at a university and quickly moved up the ladder and got a corner office like she wanted, and the furniture that she had picked out long before, would this not be "Mission Accomplished" for her, I asked myself. Would this not be reality? Effectively, would not this person be living her dream, regardless of how it was achieved? However, I thought that because a person could not achieve a dream without cost to self or others, there had to be life after Mission Accomplished. What this life would be, this outcome, I thought, was equally worth considering.

Is it possible to 'win' by 'losing?' Can we actually capably discern who is a leader and who is a servant? Can you let a person in and still get to where you are going on time? Can you get a promotion without getting the person ahead of you fired?

Two days before New Year's Day of 2013 I developed an infection in the gum. By midday, on New Year's Eve, it had become obvious to me that I needed to have my mouth examined. The only problem, I found out, was that every dentist on the face of the earth was on vacation. Though I could secure an appointment, I ended up coping with serious pain for three days. I was eventually seen by a dentist, and I felt relief, even before I got home from the appointment. It was a beautiful thing, given what I had endured for days. I was feeling better, and fast. I was filled with such gratitude for this profession and what the doctors and staff knew to do to help me get better. All I could think of on the way home was, 'I cannot believe that this profession has a high suicide rate.'

I thought about my experience with an infection for days, the pain with which I had coped and the knowledge that went into making me well. I came to the conclusion that the only reason a person in the profession would want to kill himself is if, as an example, he became a dentist for reasons that did not align with the job description. For instance, if a person became a dentist so that people could call him doctor, and then one day in a spat, a medical doctor told him that he was not a real doctor, and he took that to heart, this could depress him. I thought a person would have a better chance of not killing himself if he thought that his job was not any more important than that of a plumber who did not go to school let alone an Ivy League one. Okay, there is a point that I am trying to make, and I am sure that you got it. The medical doctor, like the plumber, may struggle with his own worth. In any case, if a dentist knew the difference that he made in people's lives, he might look at his condition differently.

We did not want to be in the position of being on the short end of the stick in a world where we had decided that we knew what the short end of the stick meant.

One day, I was coming out of my neighborhood, and I saw a man in his late fifties or so, cutting grass in the hot summer sun. The old man had a small landscaping business. It was a particularly hot summer afternoon, and in the brief moment that I spent at the stop sign, watching the man toil, I felt pity. I felt bad for the old man, his lot. But then, I began to question myself. Why is it that I thought I should feel sorry for this man? Did I think that my lot was better than his because I was in my fine air conditioned sports car or because I had a house in the area? Why did I think that this man wanted me to feel sorry for him? What line of thinking was this in which I had defined my worth by a car, a house, or not toiling in the hot summer sun?

This was an important exercise for my mind. I went further by asking myself how I would feel if that was my kid doing that type of work. Normally, I would want my kid, if I had any, to be the one that people opened doors for, a big shot. I would want my offspring to be someone who has it together, one of those 'alpha male' types. Why would I want this? I would want this because of conditions that we created, the outcome of a world that we fashioned. But could I live with it if my kid was the one that opened the door for people? Could I tolerate it? Could I let him be if he cut grass for a living? The only struggle we are in is the one with our minds. If my struggle was that I could not look at a coal miner's son the same way I would that of a neurosurgeon, could I exercise my mind? Could I bring myself to see possibilities? What other outcomes would I allow to fester; the punching of gay kids, because my mind could not tolerate it and let people be?[8]

5

MY PROBLEM WITH PERCEPTION

The message that is inherent in this book would not have been delivered any differently if it had not found a frame of reference in a government or one leader's administration. It is perhaps remarkable that it has, however. I should expect to think about and see the institutionalization of thought as a condition, an outcome, a possibility, a responsibility.

I think it was interestingly practical for our business operation for me to remind the people that I worked with that our goal was not to be nice to our guests but rather to provide service to them. Though our guests may have perceived what we did as being nice to them, we knew that this was not what we were doing. From time to time, we came to junctures that proved this point, or tested the idea; and because we knew the distinction, we tended to resolve matters in ways that educated our guests and satisfied them, even when the solution was not to their advantage.

One day at the hotel, I called two of my staff members to help me review some operational processes. I wanted to brainstorm, ask questions, and seek answers. I needed to know what others had to say about managing on a day when resources were limited. My focus was hotel public areas, and the question related to how should we arrange our cleaning priorities on a day when our resources were limited. I thought that our criteria for this arrangement of priorities should be which area a guest or anyone who visited the hotel saw first.

After some back and forth using the criteria that I provided, I came up with the order in which I thought that the common areas should be cleaned. Unbeknownst to me, one of the two staff members with whom I was having the conversation, staff member A, went to the staff member who was responsible for cleaning those areas for that day, staff member C, to give a heads-up on the order in which we should clean public areas. Shortly after that, however, staff member A looked me up and urged me to rethink my order. Staff member A made the point that if we considered the criteria thoroughly, which we all agreed was a strong and useful guideline in the situation, the order of which area got cleaned first should be different than the one I suggested. We all looked it over again, and I agreed that the order should be the one that staff member A suggested.

This, however, is what happened next. Staff member C complained that staff member A was being bossy. Apparently, Staff member A had gone back to Staff member C after our reconsideration to revise, or help revise, how Staff member C should arrange what got cleaned first. I could not understand where Staff member C got the impression that staff member A was trying to be anyone's boss. It could be that Staff member A chose words which terribly offended Staff member C, or even maybe Staff member A set out early that morning hoping to achieve the one single goal of making Staff member C feel like a subordinate.

This, however, is what I do know about the situation. What I do know is that we went from the goal of how we could operate our business so that regardless of the challenges a day might bring, we could achieve our goal of giving every guest and visitor a reason to come back to a conversation about who had more authority than whom.

What I have said is that for any condition in which we may find ourselves, there is always already something, a veil, an obstacle, a foggy screen that separates us from what we think or what we read of a situation, and what actually is or what is to be made of it.

Recently, I was hanging out with some friends. In between watching Chelsea and Bayern Munich duke it out in the EURO championship, we were able to engage one another in exciting conversations. At one point, I asked if it was possible for us to make clear, informed, objective decisions. I certainly was not trying to ask if it was possible for us to be right, let alone be right all the time. The answer that a friend gave did make the point that I was trying to highlight, which was more so a focus on what is possible. My friend said that it would be difficult for us to begin to act objectively simply because we were emotional beings.

This is not what I heard though. I thought that my friend was saying there is something wrong with us and there is nothing we could do about it. I thought my friend was saying that if he saw an advertisement on the television about a politician having an illegitimate child, he would be helpless in whether he believed the advertisement or not or even unable to decide whether or not to vote for the politician in the future. I thought that my friend was saying, "it is what it is." After reading that stereotyping is what a person does when he is too tired to dig and find accurate information, I thought that it would not be difficult for my friend to subscribe to the saying: The more specific you are, the more credible you sound.

If what a person decided to do was spend time developing the skills on how to be more specific and not how to be more accurate, it would not be the end of the world. If what a person wanted to do was spend time trying to look and sound the part rather than invest in self and expand skill set and knowledge base, this might not destroy a company. If the boss completely had the wrong perception and ended up firing the one person in the office who diligently did his job, it would not matter. It would not be the end of the world if this person and his family suffered hardship only because somebody else wanted his position and succeeded in the scheme to get it. It would not be the end of the world, but could anyone affected take the time to ponder the possibilities?

It would not be the end of the world if a person decided to base is life and his views on his own assessment of things. This is what I have said originally. And what I have also said is that the only struggle we are in is the one with ourselves, individually, with no one else involved. If a person decided that he never wanted to go near a gym let alone go from lifting a ten-pound weight one day to a fifty pound or a hundred-pound weight down the road, it would be okay. It would be his condition. Well, it would be our condition, too.

If we agreed that when a person said, "your reality is not my reality," he is more or less saying, "your perception is not my perception," then we could conclude that everyone had his or her slant on reality, or that we all had a prism through which we viewed the world.

In other words, we might expect that a person who had to walk five miles every morning to fetch water for daily necessities would see the world differently from another person who had portable water under the roof. The simple fact that their everyday lives involved different sets of real-life encounters alone should compel us to expect that they would see life differently. In fact, we might expect distinct perspectives from two different people who may have shared a similar experience.

In any case, that two people have different angles on something should be expected, after all, no two people are alike. If the one person who walked five miles to fetch water grew up to become a renowned philanthropist who advocated on behalf of the poor and needy, we might guess that such generosity was borne out of personal experience. And if a person who grew up in a privileged household failed to be sensitive to the plight of the downtrodden, it would be easy to think that if he had experienced hardship, he would have had a different perspective.

One way or another, I acknowledge that what we act out as individuals is based entirely on perception. It dictates how we interact with others and with society as a whole and as a result, it is reality, not just our reality, but reality period.

Companies invest time and money toward marketing in order to revamp their image, repackaging their brand, or maybe launching a product. Their hope in this process is growth by winning over new consumers and keeping current ones. In most, if not all cases, their goal is to impress something upon the consumer. Politicians hire strategists who carefully carve out their candidate's path toward an elected office. They are compelled by perception to construct a narrative about their candidates whom they think will appeal to the electorate. And in reality, when a candidate is elected, it is not whether the narratives were accurate, true or false, but rather whether a perception is bought and a candidate is elected.

So, suffice it to say that reality is not truth. And equally that truth is not a necessary component in our realities.

A cop who had arrested one too many black kids might start to think that every black person he met was a criminal. He might allow such experiences to become a prism through which he saw the world, and he might not think he had to excuse himself for it. That is the way he saw the world, and we had to respect it. Right?

A woman who navigates the process of natural selection with the image of her abusive alcoholic father is entitled to her reality, and we must respect it. Right? And if she naturally selects a man who has never had a drink in his life, that's a reality, including the reality of the many who are not selected because of their love for the fermented.

The gentleman who is not selected by the lady, the black man who is perceived to be a criminal; all these people are impacted by other people's reality. A person recounting a story of having run into a Good Samaritan is a beneficiary of another's reality. The bank teller who looks at a client with a $200,000.00 balance in his checking account has a perception of the individual. This, as most might think now, is reality because real things will come from how she thinks of him.

My issue is not to argue if we should use perception and reality interchangeably. My point is that if the issue the mind has is that it is not trying at all, the same way that a mind creates stereotypes because it is too lazy to find out what it to know, we should at least know this.

My point is that in all of a man's life, there is always something that stands to obscure his view; there is always something that stands to prevent him from seeing something the way that thing is to be seen. Sometimes it is his eyesight; sometimes it is the lighting in the room; sometimes it is experiences that have shaped his thinking. However a person sees an object or an idea or a situation, for whatever reason, is perfectly fine, but can he imagine what is possible, for instance if he puts on a pair of glasses?

Perception is not reality. Perception is the distance between what we have thought and what is to be thought. The question remains, though, if a person is willing to do what it takes to close that distance, or if he will prefer to say that his eyes are fine.

6

THIS IS NOT ABOUT ME

President Barack Obama often says that his administration is not about him. I cannot recall any leader in history who has said this sort of thing so many times and in so many ways. I do not see a leader who laments such an important message that very soon he will be gone, it will be finished, but what sort of outcomes can we continue to create without him.

One early Saturday morning, I called the hotel to plug in. I wanted to know what the day would look like operationally, and make my recommendations on how things should go, how best we could put the resources available to us that day to use, including our personnel. When I called back to the hotel hours later to inquire how things were going, I realized that the recommendations that I had made, specifically on who would play what role for the day, was not followed. Because I needed to know why my recommendation was not followed, I left a message for the associate involved to call me.

I needed to know why my staff did not follow my recommendations, not because it was important to me that they followed my instructions. I needed to know what we ended up doing so that I could take notice of what else worked. I was quite aware that in any given situation, I may not have made the most useful judgment, for any number of reasons. This acknowledgement was the reason that I looked at the instructions that I left for the staff as recommendations, suggestions, really. Because I had invested a great deal in finding what worked for our business operation, I held my staff to a certain endless rigor, a mind exercise in possibilities for success. I did not take this lightly.

I got the call, and the explanation presented for why we did not use people in the roles I had recommended was this: "I just did not think it was fair to let one person do all the work and another person to walk around and do nothing." What my associate thought was that the role I had given one person meant more work than the role I had given to another person. Now, because I was a little irritated, yes I am human, that what I did not hear in my associate's reasoning was how we achieved daily objectives by using staff members in their areas of strength, or looking at cost as a driver, rather than whom we liked; I needed to be emphatic. So, I said this to my associate: "Did you think that when I woke up this morning, and the first thing I thought about was the hotel, and I called to see how things went and how we could make the best of the day in front of us; did you think what I devised then in those early-morning hours was how to make one person do all the work and another person walk around and do nothing?"

My associate got my point. My associate acknowledged that it was not about me. My associate realized that I did not get off that day by getting out of bed, looking at myself in the mirror and saying to my reflection, "People had better comply with my recommendations." My associate realized that it did not matter to me who made the decision. Around me, any of us could be the boss but only by recognizing the tremendous responsibility for the possibilities that we could create.

We live in a world where we experience deadlock not because we are dealing with processes that are difficult to understand, but because one person does not want the other person to win. We live in a world where solutions are not so far out of reach, but one where we simply have not begun to exercise our minds on the idea of what is possible.

I purchased some nose guards for an associate who was allergic to smoke. This was years back when smoking rooms were still common in hotel establishments. At some point, I had replaced the nose guard because the employee reported it missing. But then, one day, this same associate came to tell me that the new nose guard which I had purchased was missing again. Someone apparently took it from the housekeeping cart. Befuddled, I wondered aloud, "How do you think you figured into this whole thing, into what becomes of the nose guard that I keep purchasing and handing to you?"

I tell the people I manage that it is highly unlikely that I am more than fifty percent responsible in a situation. Forget it. I do not do this to be unreasonable with people. I do not do this so that I could have fewer responsibilities. I have done this because of the type of outcome or the type of condition that I see is possible for my business environment.

I have seen the type of possibility that could be created in an environment where people were quick to say, 'nobody told me that.' Because this is not the sort of outcome I would want in my workplace, my staff knew that they could not say this around me. People say nobody told me that simply because they do not want to be responsible. Of all the things that could come to a person's mind about a situation at hand, the only reason a person would say that no one told him to do something is not because he is thinking he can't believe he didn't think of it on his own. A person who is quick to say that nobody told him to do something wants to be given a list of things to do, that way if something does not get done, he could say that was because it was not on the list.

I have considered that there was no way I would be able to list every scenario a person could run into in a work environment so that when the situation arose, the person could look on the list and proceed with the rewritten recommendation. Furthermore, there is a dimension to what I do that I like to think is more than myself, that I would like to think would require input from people I worked with from time to time, and if they just wanted a list, then I could not say that they were as invested as I was. I just knew it was not going to work.

The people I work with know that it will cost them something to work with me.

We had a situation whereby on the north side of the building, people were cooking out and drinking. They were also littering on the field. After several days of witnessing this behavior, my staff and I huddled to talk about it. One of us suggested that we needed to put a trash receptacle in the area. I concluded that it was a great idea, but that this was not the problem. I thought that the reason a person would litter had nothing to do with if there was a trash bin in the area. I thought that the willingness of a person not to want to pay any price would be the reason to say, for instance, that the reason he littered was because there was not a trash can in the area for him to put the trash in.

I think about the management concept that encourages to praise in public and counsel in private. Who thought this up? No. This is the sort of behavior that I have alluded to in different ways. **This is not**

about me, but it is not about you, either. Who is the person who would want you to praise him in public but counsel him only in private? Why? What does it cost this person when he has done something that called for coaching? Nothing?

In what is possible for my workplace, I could create an environment where people were good at who was going to get blamed when things did not get done, and I could create another alternative where a person knew that there was absolutely no way that he was not connected and partly responsible when something did not get done.

Most people just want to go to work, do their job, and go home. They do not want to know more than they need to; they do not want to do more than they have to. They just want to do their job and go home.

At my work, people cannot wait to get to work because they see what is possible at work. Everyone at work already knows where the other is strong and where he is weak because all of it gets talked about in public. The people that I work with look after me when I go to the store because I am not good at checking items for the expiration date. It helps me a great deal because I do not have to have walls around me about the things that I do not do well. It also makes me better at the things that I am not good at because people already know I am bad at it. The only way for me is up.

At my work, if a person wants to be the boss - to take charge and make decisions for the workplace, it is in my best interest to let the person step in and be the boss. If my idea does not work, I want it out of there. This is a cost to me. I do not want you to tell me that my idea works when it does not. I do not want to tell myself that my idea works when it does not. If someone else's idea is better than mine, I want this to be clear to everyone.

This is an outlook that means that I do not give people "an out" at my job. It simply is not the sort of outcome I want to create. I just think that there is something incredibly useless, or rather harmful to society, about it. I do not find that a person can create different possibilities if he knows that there is no cost to him. Why would I want to give a person an out? How would that be useful for him? How would it be practical in the workplace?

Right now in society, we do not want people to feel embarrassed. We let them down gently. As a result, we have created an outcome where people continue to say incredibly outrageous things without cost to them. They become emboldened, without any hope that these people would go home and look at themselves in the mirror and ponder the things that they say and how they contributed to society. This has not happened, so we are all responsible for the possibilities this is robbing us of creating.

I find it to be a historic marker that we have a leader in this world who keeps saying, "This is not about me. I did not come here for me. I came for what is possible." There are outcomes that we create now but can we begin to exercise our minds on what else is possible? Can we begin to believe that it is possible for this journey to not be about us and to see what outcomes that could create?

7

A SIDE AND THE TEST OF TIME

America is an exceptional country. I do not mean this in a way that a person who has something to say about heart health may find himself tangled up in a conversation with someone who sees substance in whether or not potatoes should be mashed. Even more precisely, I do not mean this in the way that I observed as I listened to Sean Hannity and others take issue with Supreme Court Justice Ruth Bader Ginsburg and her thought about the guidance emerging new societies should seek in drafting their constitution.⁹ I do not see this through a who-am-I-better-than lens. America is an exceptional country because she fights with herself. She represents everything about a human being. She represents best what a human being is. She can be beautiful. She can be maddening. She can be dark. She can be inspiring. She imagines. She tries. This is why she has always been ahead, good or bad. I find this to be admirable.

In writing this book, I see the intersection of where a country or society could take itself and the possibility that the mind would emerge as the final frontier. It is what we are able to do with the mind that prevails. This in itself is a matter of what is possible because we could elect to embrace using the discovering of our minds as a tool for outcomes for society, or we could shun it all together.

In a way, with the election of Barack Obama, I am tempted to think about how appropriate it may seem that the country that has led the world in most ways would position itself for the battle which would emerge, the battle of the capable mind. If we were faced with the thought that what the mind could create would be the only thing that remained in the end, we could once again say that America was ahead for having elected a mind like that of Barack Obama.

The event that is the election and reelection of not just an African American individual to the presidency, but also an individual who by consensus busies his mind, is a struggle that is evident in the intense ideological events that have marked with this presidency. This itself not only represents the fight I spoke of, but also a society's own instincts about what prevails. Since the election of Mr. Obama to the presidency, we have had to wonder if corporations were people, too. We have had a contentious debate, whether one person with health insurance should worry about another person without it. We have seen a line of thought that making the process intrusive and sub-human might cause a person to rethink having an abortion. And the high-minded idea of a person's right to vote without hurdles to clear has been brought to the forefront for reconsideration.

In all this, I have thought that we may be witnessing our best chance to change the conversation completely. We may have for the first time the clear chance to look at the role that thinking plays as central to what is possible in society. That in an institutional sort of way, we may go from not asking any questions at all, to asking ourselves one or two questions, to using our minds to sort out weighty and difficult ideological questions, to actually seeing this as the order of the day.

Consider a community where the degree to which the people in that community were able to interact with their environment and understand it and discover what was possible with their daily existence was based on how physically fit they were. Consider also, and quite evidently, that this was not a community that you would consider fit by any stretch of the imagination. Though it would not be the end of the world, the reality that the folks in this community would be capable of creating on a daily basis would be different from the one that they would be able to create if most of them are New York Marathon or decathlon competition worthy.

Whether we like it or not, we are faced daily with a test. We must answer the question regarding what sort of reality we are capable of creating, and what kind of outcomes we are fit to fashion? In what ways are we able to sort out the challenges of the day? Are we as fit as those challenges that the changing society is creating for us to confront every waking moment?

If you run a business where people lift fifty pound boxes and all the associates you have hired can only lift twenty five pounds, your business reality will be of a certain sort. For instance, every time an associate has to lift a box, he will have to find another associate to help. The time it takes to deliver service as a result of your associates strength may suffer. Your business will look a certain way; it will have a certain reality or outcome as a result. Of course, you can change that outcome – what your collective daily life and business operation looks like – by putting your staff

on a strength and conditioning regimen so that each staff member finds himself eventually able to lift a fifty pound box.

Ultimately, we can do whatever we want. We actually can. It is important for people to know this. This is not a fight. It is important for us to be clear minded about this. The substantive point to make, the test-of-time point to make, is that we can do whatever we want. We could collect all the guns our little hearts desire. We could fall in love with the robots that we build. We could abort all the kids we want. We could invent gadgets that would allow us to not have to interact with another human being ever again. We could do any ethnic cleansing that we found justifiable. If a government decided to control the airwaves in order to influence what its people think about anything, it would not be the end of the world. This book is not an argument.

There is only one thing that is going to prevail in the end. The only thing that will prevail in the end is thought, and particularly, its caliber. For instance, we could begin a dialogue on the likelihood that it is not what a person looks like or what he wears, or what he drives, that makes him who he is, but rather, it is what a man says, it is the words that come out of his mouth, that defines him. We could come up with this thought, take this position, and see where it takes us. We could sleep on this and see what happens in the morning. We could see what happens, a week later or a decade later.

On the subject of sleep, a person might not have to wonder for a good while whether he required it or not. At eight or nine or ten in the morning, a person might be consumed with doing other things like running, going to work at a local college, sitting on the porch and wondering about the big orange glow ball emerging from the east. If this person encountered a sleep antagonist, by noon, he might begin to think that he did not need sleep. And quite possibly because it was noon, he could afford this luxury. Imagine that.

Even if he was persuaded two hours later by a sleep advocate, someone who could give a compelling argument why our friend would find that he required sleep, he still could afford not to justify anything or show any rigor in his sympathy for one position or the other. In fact, he literally would have all day to come up with his own advocacy on the matter of sleep. He would have this room to not have to give an account. He could say that sleep was necessary, but only an hour of it, while the body was suspended in the air upside down.

There would be a whole day to talk about sleep, to research it. We could be diligent about what position to take about whether it was needed or not. We could make up anything about it in pure speculation while still holding an audience. At four and five and six in the evening, the debate would rage on. Then, three, or four, or five hours later, a juncture begins to emerge for the person who had wondered whether he needed sleep or not. Just while he was succumbing to the idea that he indeed required sleep, the sleep antagonist showed up, slipped our friend a pill that would keep him up for days. In the days that followed, our friend remained a skeptic. Sooner, however, he realized that this position was not sustainable for him.

Like I have alluded to, the event that is the presidency of Mr. Barack Obama has created more useful junctures than perhaps any other time in history has in terms of lessons on what is possible, on what prevails, on where the mind can take itself.

I watched Pat Robertson, the Christian Leader, on television not long ago. What he said addressed an issue that I think about often, one that I thought I could share in this book. By the way, allow me to remark that I have not cited examples in this book or told of my experiences so that I could call attention to people, including myself. I hope that what we take away are lessons and ideas. The people, including myself, pale in relation to the lessons to convey. We are not talking about or focused on people; we are focused on concepts or ideas. I could have been the one who said any of the ideas discussed. We are only interested in the ideas so that we can put their utility to the test and see if we can learn anything.

I may not have said that the best way possible. What I am trying to say is that I hope no one finds himself or herself the focus of anything that I have said, or that I will say in this book. This would be unfortunate simply because my interest is not to call attention to people. Any of us could have been the reason that we talk about a particular outcome or condition.

The point that I am trying to make is that I hope we do not find ourselves in a situation, an outcome, not unlike one where one person goes to another person and says, "You have problems, nineteen of them to be exact. I can tell you some of these problems that you have but you probably already know about them. Just go on and handle your business and let me know how I can help." After all this, the person with the problem looks at his friend and says, "I do not like the way you talk to me."

Anyway, back to what I had to say about a comment from the Christian Leader, as he is referred to. This is what Mr. Robertson said:

Your country will be torn apart by internal stress. A house divided cannot stand. Your president holds a radical view of the direction of your country, which is at odds with the majority. Expect chaos and paralysis. Your president holds a view which is at the odds with the majority — it's a radical view of the future of this country, and so that's why we're having this division. This is a spiritual battle which can only be won by overwhelming prayer. The future of the world is at stake because if America falls, there's no longer a strong champion of freedom and a champion of the oppressed of the world. There must be an urgent call to prayer.[10]

As I listened to Mr. Robertson make this claim, I could only think of one possibility, and I know you are thinking it too: what if God, the one Mr. Robertson speaks of, shows up and goes, "Whoa, whoa, you got that wrong. That Obama dude, yeah, yeah, that's my guy. You have to realize sometimes that your ways are not like mine."

I think about this in the same way that I ponder how anyone who has ever done anything in the name of a God they profess should think about the things that they do on His behalf. There is the likelihood that their God might show up and say, "You are absolutely not representing me right now." I have wondered if anyone has thought about this as a responsibility, and of course, a colossal embarrassment when the mark is missed.

If, for the sake of analogy, America had its own God, one that was not Socialist or Marxist or Fascist or Muslim or one that would never have endorsed anyone not born in the United States, and after Obama's terms, the clouds opened up and that God revealed that Obama was his guy, and he was never any one of those things we called him, I wonder if any single one of those who said all those things about him would go home and look in the mirror and say, "The only struggle I am in is the one with my mind, a struggle for which I alone am responsible, and that I alone have to sort out." Would it not be interesting if after his terms, Mr. Obama returned to that same God?

In what ways could one person convince another that he was not the other? In what ways could the person who knew show the person who did not know that he did not know?

These are not questions that we need to answer. It will not be useful to answer such questions. Every day, we create outcomes, conditions, based on the potency of our minds. A useful starting point, however, is for us to acknowledge that the reason we act the way we do is that we are not intelligent enough to act otherwise.

If it turns out that what we are witnessing is monumental, and if it becomes evident that what we have seen are conversational and ideological landmarks, and if it turns out that this man, on whose account, we have said things, or that so much has been revealed, is actually one of us, where does that leave us? Where does it leave what we think about when we go to bed at night, if we have such a thing?

One day, I was watching The Daily Show by a certain Jon Stewart. In the episode, one of the correspondents, Aasif Mandvi, shows up at a news conference where Florida Governor Rick Scott is to present budget recommendations. Mr. Mandvi's unrelated request was to have the governor pee in a cup to show that he was not on drugs. I suspect that Mr. Mandvi's logic was that since the governor had proposed a law that required welfare recipients to submit to drug testing to qualify for state benefits, and since the governor and his administration is equally at the mercy of taxpayer dollars, the governor himself was not above such a drug test.[11]

It is possible that a person who has found himself in a position of authority may fail to see how much he has in common with a fellow man who is far removed from such privilege. It was remarkable that the request by Mr. Mandvi is an exercise for the governor to see how similar he is to a welfare recipient. I may have digressed.

I cannot fault anyone for what he may have done or what he may represent in human history. Everyone thinks that he is right. If, however, any of us would end up looking through the eyes of history and wishing for a different outcome, if we would find ourselves agreeing with what a person said ten, or fifteen years earlier, we should wonder if it would be possible to find a way to agree sooner.

If what we have institutionally is an opportunity for a different exercise for the mind, or exercise for the mind for the first time, if what we are witnessing is the likelihood that we would at least inescapably see, through the divergence in ideologies that the presidency of Barack Obama has created, that there are other outcomes that we could create, then when all is said and done, we will have known beyond doubt that we are capable of creating more possibilities different than the ones that we currently know.

THE BARACK OBAMA JUNCTURE

3 ON WHAT IS RIGHT

The reason we act the way we do is that we are not intelligent enough to act otherwise. This is like saying that the reason a person is not able to lift a dumbbell of a certain weight is that he is not strong enough to do so.

As a reminder, if I have not articulated it already, my objective in writing this book is not to criticize or complain or condemn anyone or anything. Everybody is fine. If a person thinks that the way to find out what is inside the pages of a book is to strap the book to his forehead, this is fine. We are not judges. If a person thinks that his way is the right way, no problem. However, for everyone who has thought or believed anything, there is a burden.

A person who thinks that he is right has the same burden as the one he places on the person that he thinks is wrong. How? Both of them still have to wonder what is possible beyond what they have thought. Why? Because whatever a person thinks is really just an idea of a certain weight and what is obvious is that there is always a weight heavier than the one a person is able to lift. There is always another idea worth exercising beyond the one a person has exercised.

Where the rubber meets the road is that ideas that we think or manufacture and demonstrate make the world look the way it does. It would appear then, again, that all our energy should go toward what sort of thoughts or ideas we are able to manufacture or espouse.

On this note, we need to determine or define the role that money should play in our lives. We need to know the meaning or value that we should ascribe to it, and what place it occupies. I am convinced that this will reveal profound possibilities for how we conduct ourselves and how we act. I cannot think of a greater driver for the possibilities that we are capable of creating, certainly on the level of Ethics, than the one based on our view of money.

I saw a bumper sticker that read: The Time To Do The Right Thing Is Now. This is a thought that I have trouble digesting simply because I do not think that our interest should be to want to, at any juncture, categorize what we do as 'right.' Since the reason we act the way we do is that we are not intelligent enough to act otherwise, we would practically be setting ourselves up for complications by thinking that the end game is to be able to say that an act is right or that it is wrong.

One evening at a social gathering of an international nature, I was having light hearted conversations with friends from around the globe. A friend had jokingly followed up to something that I said with, "Common Christian, do you not trust me?" To this question I equally lightheartedly responded, "I am not in the business of trust." My point is that a useful starting point for us is not to try to pose questions that may not be there or that we may be unable to answer.

I have concluded that there is yet a unique possibility that we could create. I thought that it was not necessary to ponder whether our actions were right or not. I thought that we could be less concerned about how we acted and more concerned about the nature of what might be driving how we acted.

In other words, not having the right perspective on something, anything, for that matter, could create disasters of unspeakable proportions. It can create defects.

One day at work, someone saw smoke coming out of the guest laundry room and assumed that a dryer that was in use had caught on fire. This assumption was acted upon without any investigation, and the hotel was evacuated. It turned out that the smoke was from an overloaded washer with an overworked motor and burned belt.

I have seen people lose their lives on the way to being the first to lay claim to a flat-screen television at a department store on Black Friday. How we should act is the least of my concerns.

The most important endeavor we face is one where we have properly assessed a situation, an object, or a condition. Can we think the appropriate thought in a situation?

A recent article that I wrote addresses such sentiment. Here is the article:

I was in a hotel room on the morning of the 15th of December, 2010 getting ready for the day. I was also getting a dose of Morning Joe in which Rick Stengel, managing editor at Time Magazine was a guest. On this morning, Mr. Stengel was there to announce Mark Zuckerburg of Facebook as Time Magazine person of the year. Mr. Stengel remarked, I supposed in defending Time Magazine's choice, that the way we relate with one another in the future would forever be influenced, or perhaps determined, by phenomenon such as Facebook.

Perplexed, I began to ponder not if but how Facebook, the social networking website where people go to talk about themselves, and post videos, and share files, will change the way we relate with one another. I thought there was a chance that this analysis was only as profound as announcing that the utility of the automobile will be forever changed, determined by the introduction of cars with folding side view mirrors. It was evident that this was a phenomenon that we would need to categorize its impact.

On days in the classroom, when most might worry about how to reach an elementary school student with learning and behavioral issues that may be traced to home and living conditions; on the day of a precarious helicopter rescue mission at sea of people, some of them with small babies; on a day that a researcher quietly arrives in his laboratory to resume a complex research that has taken years and with no breakthrough in sight; the people at Facebook are having a meeting on changing or revamping the message service on Facebook.[12] This is an effort that has its place, but where is that place?

This obviously is not an attempt to be critical of Facebook, or even to start a debate on whether Mr. Zuckerburg's work is man-of-the-year material. The point to observe is if Time Magazine, and the rest of society at large, and by that I mean adults, have thought of and acknowledged first, that we need to be able to contextualize the conversations and the things that we call phenomena. The challenges that we face are so glaringly fundamental. The measure is not how massively we connect or even gather. This cannot be a reasonable starting point. I submit that the useful starting point is not how many people were able to gather, but rather what they talked about.

Do not get me wrong; there is something worth noting in technological acceleration, but only in the same way that you appreciate it if you had one of those remote car lock activators on a rainy day, and you are coming out of the grocery store without an umbrella and with hands full of grocery bags. I should note that not unlike Facebook, Mr. Zuckerburg's previous project was a website where Harvard's students could compare the hotness of their peers.[13] These efforts seem like the work of an entrepreneurial mind without a doubt, and one that is worth commending. The greater point to make is if this were a piece in a puzzle, do we know where to put it?

The exercise by Time Magazine to name Mark Zuckerberg man of the year and the article that was written about it were probably focused on writing articles. It may have been focused on selling magazines by talking about common things that we are used to finding in articles, like 'Zuckerberg tries to put himself in the heads of people who don't have his weapons-grade mental hardware, his immunity to peer pressure, his absolute mastery of his privacy settings and his gift for inspiring loyalty.'[14]

We could liken what is happening in society to a middle age business operator who has decided to hire a young individual, a young college graduate, for instance. What the statesman would find in the young addition to his team, and hopefully he has made an excellent hire in a bright young associate, is infectious enthusiasm and an active mind with myriad ideas. Of course, there are two experiences that will be at play here that are both based on the abilities of the business operator. The first experience is that if the business operator were a competent and forward thinking individual, he would find his associate's ideas to be sometimes already tried and tested, sometimes good, and sometimes plain youthful.

I submit in this scenario that the youth would be better off in the future, as would the business, with a serious, intellectual, and experienced business owner who can mold, confer with, and challenge a youthful mind. These are all my own digressive arguments, considering that I was first inspired to look at the Time Magazine article in a way to imply that the only people we have in society to whom to defer are adults.

Now, if the manager is a mediocre business operator who had not thought, let alone tried, half the ideas in the world for his business, he might deem most ideas from his new associate original and relevant. In this case, neither the youth nor the business is better off in the long run. The youth would gain confidence and influence for positions that were not tried, tested, scrutinized, challenged, or thought through; and the future of that business would be a different one as a result. I have said all this as a reminder that we are still talking possibilities, not right, not wrong, just what is possible.

What we have now is what we had as recently as a decade or two ago. What we have is a lack of effort and unwillingness in the pursuit of an evolving conscience. What we have still are people looking for the next "big thing." Wall Street bankers still are trying to cash in ungodly amounts from any source of revenue they can find, and professional money managers, day traders, and even young college graduates are not interested if there is consequence, just ordinary people enticed by the prospect of instant wealth.[15]

What we have is a blinded interest in continuing to create a culture that is driven by big stories, one that keeps pushing the conversation in a direction where anyone can manufacture a climate that will take advantage of our collective frivolous minds. What we have is a complete lack of moral compass that has delivered to us a world where a person has sparked our curiosity, or the lack there of, by taking an x-ray photo of her buttocks and generating news as a result. What we have now is a father's lament when he compares his interests from his teenage years, which involved tinkering with appliances and figuring out how things worked, to the interests of his two teenage daughters. It is the adults in the room who have failed to present to the younger generation that they at least have an idea what the future should look like.

At any point in time, it will be up to the older generation to start the conversation in the attempt to find where things go. It will be up to the older generation to show a level of substance that will steer the younger generation away from an inability to know what is important and what is not. We need the older generation to explain that it is not whether people are able to get together and connect on a massive scale that is important; it is what they talk about and the ability to have life-changing discourse that matters. The phenomenon is in knowing that what we talk about is what matters, just as the discernment is not left to the fresh member of a business but rather the responsibility of the veteran business operator.

We need the older generation to prepare us for what the health of our moral compass means for the future, and to convince us that there is inevitable consequence and that our ability to find the equilibrium need rest in wise, steady hands. We need adults to convey to us that our most important job is to be more intelligent and for them to set us on a course away from a preoccupation with nonentities.

Objectively, I really could not say that adults owed anything to anybody in the way of possibly explaining how things worked. This would require that there was a way things worked, and that adults actually knew it.

My whole point is that there is a separate preoccupation that involves knowing what anything means, where anything falls, or what role anything plays. And knowing this becomes a matter of possibilities because it requires the workings of the mind.

If a person buys a car and one day discovers how convenient it is to unlock it and even open up the trunk by lifting up his foot while holding bags of groceries in heavy down pour, and then he decides that not having this should keep him up at night the same way that he is kept up at night when he gets into a verbal altercation with his college-age son who storms out of the house and does not return for the night, this would not be the end of the world. It would only be the case that different possibilities are created.

Often when I am at the traffic light, I think about the idea of being at the light. I think about the times that I am the first at the traffic light. I think about it when I am two, three, or fifteen cars deep. I think about the times when I am so far back, I know that I would not catch the light. Before I get further into the various things that I think about the human experience that is being at the traffic light, I would like to start with the acknowledgement that there is a different possibility that we could create if we all come up to the light with the mindset that we would want to be the first at the light.

Now, we could observe, as a useful starting point, that we would not all be the first to get to the traffic light, not all the time at least. We would not all make it to the traffic light at the same time. This is an outcome I personally have acknowledged.

It would be evident, and interesting, the sort of outcome that would be created if it happens that each of us is bent on making it to the traffic light first.

Nevertheless, I opt to think that we would not all make it to the traffic light at the same time. There is always going to be the fellow who arrives first at the light. There would be the second person and the third. There would be the person who would not catch the light and would have to wait another turn.

All this said, it would be counter intuitively fascinating if somehow we decided to put value, I mean of the kind that is coveted, on getting to the light first.

This would create an incredibly compelling outcome. An outcome, presumably, and because the focus is on getting to the light first, that could orient some to think that the key is in the type of car driven, how fast it is, for instance. With a focus on getting to the traffic light first, some might devise a method that would prevent others, or one that circumvents their natural order. Others might find partnerships that would give them an advantage in a team network sort of way, one that might cause them to think, "Let us control who gets to the light. Let us give ourselves an advantage."

In a society where it is all about who gets to the light first, where your status is based on how many times you have gotten to the light first, getting to the light first could become a serious occupation.

Whether anyone takes the time to wonder where getting to the light first fits in the grand scheme of everything that defines life for the people in this society is an inevitable thought. Regardless of how long it takes to ponder this, however, much would be made of the pursuit of getting to the light first.

Some people might think that it would take getting up early and getting ready to be able to get to the light first. The extent to which such perspective might shape a person's life is in itself open to possibilities. A person who is a deep sleeper might go out and purchase multiple alarm clocks in order to ensure that he woke up at a set time. He might go out and purchase a new mattress in hope that whatever amount of sleep he got on any given night was quality sleep. This would set him up to wake up energetically, and improve his chances of getting to the light first.

Others might believe that the key to getting to the light first had to be in the type of car that a person drove. For most, this could create life-changing outcomes. A person who thought that he needed a certain fast car, by his definition, but who did not have one would have to devise a way to get one. This could change his condition significantly. The person then might be focused on how the car is driven as a component to getting to the light first. With this as well, there is a lot that could happen in the way this individual operated his vehicle with getting to the traffic light first on his mind.

Further, there are those who would become convinced that getting to the light first could not be done without some sort of an elaborate scheme. So, a person might take time to study traffic light technology and how to rig it. He might get his friends to help him manipulate how and when the light changed with a promise of sharing in whatever status is bestowed upon him in the aftermath of his notoriety. This person might study patterns of who his competitors were on any given day and any given time of the day and figure that his best chances rested in disabling or sabotaging those who could stand in the way.

All this had happened because somehow a society decided that the real deal, the important thing, what obtained, was getting to the traffic light first.

There are those who would look at getting to the light first as something that they accomplished on their own. They did that. A person might even find ways to disregard the time when the reason he ended up in the front was because the car ahead of him broke down. The person might begin to develop a certain complex around getting to the light first, especially if he had managed to do this a number of times. In fact, if he was of the persuasion that the car one drove determined if you got to the light first or not, he might look at people of whose vehicles he has not approved and regard them as those who stood no chance of getting close to the light, let alone being the first at it.

Of course, there are those who would say that the reason they had trouble getting to the light first was because of the vehicle that they drove, the one that had trouble starting in the cold. They might say that it was because of living condition - the one that did not include a sleep number bed, relaxation music on a zero harmonic distortion sound system, a good shower before bed, and a properly air conditioned environment. A person who had not been to the traffic light first might begin to think that there was a conspiracy against him. He might begin to look at those who have enjoyed first-at-light status a time or two with resentment. This dynamic also creates a condition for the society.

The only struggle we are in is the one with our minds, each of us, individually, with no one else involved. This struggle, of course, has a component to it that wants to ask us about what is a proper course of action. The question of how one should act in this situation that man will find himself asking is one that is not without context. I wonder though of the outcomes we end up creating depending on whether we start out defining concepts of what is right and what is wrong.

There are so many outcomes that we could create around getting to the traffic light first. We could camp out there and not do other things. We could find ways to create an advantage for ourselves at the expense of other people. We could jostle for it, perhaps from a mile out, sometimes creating a massive pile up that involved loss of lives and tied-up traffic for hours.

Whatever value we may have given to getting to the traffic light first, we could also acknowledge that we would not all get to the traffic light at the same time. We could make this evident. We could make it evident that a useful outcome would be to get as many cars through the light as possible once it turned green. We could take this seriously enough that everyone paid attention to the light. We could take this seriously enough that it would be unacceptable to us that the reason we did not get enough cars through was because a driver was picking his nose and not paying attention to the light, or maybe he was on the phone - not saving a life somewhere but talking about who is sleeping with whom. Those could be outcomes to avoid.

We could take this seriously enough that when a person did not make it through the light, he was not angry at the people who did. He was not left with the feeling that somebody was after him or that somebody did not want him to succeed by making it through the light. This because it would be evident to those who did not make it through the light that everyone ahead who made it had the interest of others at heart. As soon as the light turned green, it was go-go-go. No one relaxed as he approached the intersection, even upon realizing he would make it through the light. He continued expediently so that as many more behind could make it as well.

We could do this in such a way that left others who did not make it through the light with a satisfactory feeling that those who did tried their best, that those who did had them in mind all along. We could do this not in a way that some walked around with an I-made-it-through-the-light complex. We could consider an outcome that did not pitch those who made it through the light against those who did not in a finger pointing mindset that it was because some wanted it enough, and others did not. We could do this in a way that the person who had not made it through the light recognized the role that he played in the equilibrium that is possible, one that would involve him not demonizing those who made it through. This would be an exercise for the mind. Such exercise would be the same that a person who was not happy with his camper but wanted someone else's camper would have to do. The reason being that society, including the individual whose camper is coveted, would have a reason to say, "My camper should not become a problem. I am happy with my camper, but can you be happy with yours?"

The only struggle we are in is the one with our minds, each of us, individually, with no one else involved.

We could create an outcome where it is obvious that not everyone will make it to the light first, but everyone can be okay with it because everyone is doing his best.

In my line of work, it is not only necessary but also required of me to constantly find creative ways to develop people because we recognize that the right people in the right positions is important to the overall success of our business. As a result, it is not uncommon for me to tell a story, pose a question, or share an experience in order to elicit a reaction or make a point.

On a recent exercise, I asked a few of my staff members a question for the purpose of painting a picture. The question that I asked was, "Why do you think that I would not steal?" As you might expect, I got all sorts of answers. One staff member conjectured that I would not steal because I was convinced that stealing was morally wrong. Another person said it might be that stealing was against my religious beliefs. While yet another thought that I would not steal because I was not predisposed to selfishness or to acquiring material possessions.

Soon after, it was my turn to share my view. I simply told my staff that the reason I would not steal was because it was not in my job description. I also needed to make the point that it would not be useful to think that religious beliefs or other dispositions would have anything to do with why a person would not steal.

What I have found in a lot of situations is that people unnecessarily complicate a process either by over thinking it or more often by adding other processes that are not related to or needed for completing the process at hand and achieving a desired result. For whatever motive, we tend to ignore what works by leaving the Modus Operandi manual at home. Unfortunately, such is an approach that overlooks the simple requirement for the right foundation upon which to build expertise.

I have imagined a useful exercise in which I obtained a copy of the job description for the clerk at the local gas station and studied it before going inside to pay for gas. There was a time, in fact, when I had gone inside to make a suggestion to the clerk about how he and his coworkers could improve customer service. Thinking that I was there to complain about something, he quickly started to tell me that he did not care for any complaints, just as soon as I mentioned that I had suggestions for their business. Though it was obvious that this gas-station attendant heard a lot of complaints, I am certain that nowhere in his job description did it say not to listen to his customers or to assume that they had nothing to offer but to complain about the service and product at the gas station.

A while back, I happened to be the victim of what appeared to be a prank caller determined to test my composure or drive me completely insane. I was working behind the desk at a hotel at the time. This particular night, the phone kept ringing back to back to back but each time when I answered the call, the caller would hang up.

The first few times were not a big deal. However, by the tenth and twentieth and thirtieth time that I had answered the phone only to have the caller hang up on me, I had experienced all ranges of emotions and imagined everything on the face of the earth that I could say to a ne'er-do-well. I had also seized it as an opportunity to appreciate a section in the description of what it was that my job entailed. This being, when the phone rang, I should answer it professionally using an established script with a smile in my voice and ready to be of service. As a result, it quickly became a nonissue for me that the phone was ringing back to back to back. I simply saw answering the phone as doing my job. When the phone rang, I answered it. It was not a bother to me what the intention of the caller might have been. I just kept doing my job of answering the phone. That I answered the phone some fifty times in a very short time from a caller who was probably bent on testing my patience was not my focus. My focus was that I had been hired to answer the phone whenever it rang, and that was what I did.

In a recent conversation, a friend and I agreed, from a service standpoint, that if I owned a restaurant, and he happened to patronize it, while he was in the restaurant, I would offer to him the service that I would offer to any other customer. That is, in the purest sense, it would not matter to me in that immediate environment that I knew him. He would simply be a customer hoping for the best meal and the best service and hopefully expecting that his friend's restaurant would not fail to deliver.

Though I have used examples from the service industry, we will find examples from all areas of life when it comes to how we should act. We may find that not only should we not look at our effort as a pursuit to define what is the right and what is the wrong way to act, we should be even more concerned about the premise that would drive how we end up acting.

One way or another, I would like to think that all conversations lead to this, that as humans, we should begin to regard the mind as the final frontier. And this process is not one that we will bring about, but rather one that will happen to us. The mind, on its own, will become serious enough that it will be impossible for us to ignore that which is obvious.

Allow me to conclude my thought about how we should act by sharing in this book a paper that I wrote recently on the subject of corporate malfeasance. My position at the time, my instincts on the matter, was not to look at greed as the reason for corporate scandals. I thought at the time that the pressure to perform, the value that we had placed on this, was the reason for transgressions. We created a very competitive culture around year over year growth. We make leaders who want to be seen as the turnaround experts achieve such status at any cost. This outcome that we have created is not unlike the one that a society created by placing value on getting to the traffic light first. The way people ended up acting really depended on how the traffic light event was defined.

Here is the article:

The current economic climate has given us enough to talk about when it comes to corporate corruption, and many have looked to the past for answers to the difficult situation where rampant scandalous corporate behaviors nearly brought down the world's most vibrant economy. Once we look, we see a history of an American capitalist market system that is often threatened by the tendencies of businesses and entrepreneurs to transgress in their search for capital, and we also see how regulations always stand like an antidote ready to save the market. As we examine history, we begin to wonder about the obvious cycle of collapses and near collapses of the market and if there has been an accurate diagnosis of the root cause of corporate corruption, or if there has been any attempt to look at the problem from a different angle. One such attempt is the position that the pressure to perform on the part of the business executive and the securities analyst, and the demand for performance by institutional investors and shareholders alike, is the reason for corporate malfeasance that we have seen time and again.

In looking at corporate scandals, we have to go back a century to see that what has always been at stake is the capitalist system itself, and that the use of government regulations has always been necessary as the way to preserve and improve it. The first instance of regulations intended to help preserve capitalism came in the latter part of the nineteenth century when antitrust laws were enacted in order to prevent key industries from being taken over by monopolists. Soon after that, the Great Depression of the 1920s caused by trading excesses necessitated the passage of laws collectively referred to as the New Deal. From that point on, anyone looking to raise money for business would have to show truthfully what the business would be about. The intent of this emerging dynamic between regulation, for instance, the New Deal, and capitalism itself was that free market will serve as the deterrent for those who might be tempted to transgress in the pursuit of capital (Stelzer, 2004).

The cycle of business transgressions and that of counteracting government regulations only leaves one burning question, 'Is it the system?' What appears inherent about capitalism as an economic system is the requirement for profit and hence a focus on a means to achieve it. By definition, capitalism is taking the means of production and distribution, along with labor, and manipulating them in order to realize a profit. A business in a market place will tend to want to grow its share of the market. It not only wants to increase its share so that it can increase its profit. It recognizes a second component which is that there is competition and in order to stay competitive, it has to go after its competitors. A successful business that recognizes the dynamic that every advantage is temporary maintains a proactive and offensive business strategy that as we have seen may result, for instance, in monopolistic tendencies. Generally speaking, we see that there are several different ways in which companies and businesses will manifest the innate characteristic that is needed to compete in the market. It is interesting, a testament to the unyielding way of the capitalist market, that even in the face of regulations like the passing of the Sarbanes-Oxley Act, companies were still looking for a way to make a profit. Technology companies jumped at the chance to develop accounting programs that would help companies become SOX compliant (Florian & Burke, 2003). The performance expectation imposed by the system that involves the manipulation of essential variables that are necessary in order to achieve profit gives rise at one time or another to overreach. This, one could argue, is an ongoing dynamic that has very little to do with greed, fundamentally, but rather with the composition of a vibrant system and the need to keep it balanced. So, what we see are the patterns of the capitalist economic system both in terms of its demands and the elements of its makeup. Time and again, a system that is built on the expectation of performance finds itself needing to be regulated. That is, there is a natural tendency to push the system to the brink and then there is the typical consequential result that requires regulation. Often, the storyline is one of cause and effect of a system that is built more on performance and less on the occasional scandal that is associated with a market collapse or with failure. With the backdrop of the complex nature of an economic market system, we look further at other components that expose the market to scandal, or that create the tendencies for a company to push itself to the brink. We find no other way to explain it than to look at the people who affect the system, that is, the chief executive of a company, the securities analysts who understand the economic system, and the public, or shareholders who have a stake in it all.

First, there is a tendency for the company's chief executive officer to want to show a healthy, profitable company. After all, there are other companies in the industry that are also jousting for an advantage. Failure simply is not acceptable in a competitive environment serious enough to warrant huge amounts of money to be invested in corporate espionage and market research. A certain Chief Executive for Royal Ahold, one of the world's biggest food retailers, Mr. Cees van der Hoeven, was revered because of the reputation that he turns a dull and underperforming company into a growth machine (Economist, 2003). We know that people enjoy what reputation they have for a host of reasons, and we cannot argue that those who have worked hard to cultivate a certain reputation and persona intend to maintain it, sometimes at all cost. After all, it is nice to be at the top. It is nice to be on top because those who are on top like to keep their top spot. There are other reasons that a company's chief executive might want to be so intent on showing a healthy and profitable company that relates once again to the pressure to perform. That is, society has given them a reason to look at themselves as go getters or success stories, and it is just plain difficult to have to disappoint and reveal an inadequacy. As if to imply that they have tasted the life of socialites and debutantes, those who are put in place to manage multi-million dollar companies often end up preferring their social lives over employing hard-nosed tactics in running their companies or bothering to deliver bad news when the company is not performing well.

It is not only difficult for the chief executive officer of a company to deliver bad news; it is also hard for the consumer of the news to take bad news. There is a say-it-isn't-so or a lie-to-me culture out there. Perhaps it is the abused spouse syndrome where the victim becomes an enabler, hoping it will just go away, and the good old times will return. As one writer admits, the story may be more complicated, conflicted and tragically human than all the conjectures that often emerge from the scandal news breaks (Maich, 2006). The monstrous nature and complexity of the market system reveal itself when politicians and lobbyist who at the height of the scandal voted for regulation were starting to reconsider their positions, worrying that the unintended consequence of the regulation might be a decrease in competition and innovation (New Republic, 2005). In a similar way, and as if to imply that the sky would fall and the economy would be no more if money managers were held accountable, Mary L Shapiro, then chairman of the SEC proposed unannounced inspection of 10000 money managers only to scale it back to 1600. The struggle of who is supreme between the shareholder and the corporate boards is one that even the chamber of commerce itself has called unworkable (Westbrook, 2009). It is difficult at times to gauge who loves the system more, the companies that prop it up or the rest of us who wants to see a show.

In order to stay competitive and remain profitable, there at some point has to be new and innovative ways of doing business. That is what the securities analysts and institutional investors thought and also heard; and though the Securities Analyst is seen as up to no good because of the conflict-of-interest nature of his job, the laws that are being enacted only deal with symptoms and not the cause of corporate scandals and corruption (Nott and Adjibolosoo, 2005). So, the case of the securities analyst is an interesting one. We know that conflict of interest happens when an individual is involved in multiple activities in which there is greater interest for one activity over the other. This is the life of the securities analyst, and the dynamic itself, we would all agree, does not make the individual partial. However, judging by the fact that conflict of interest is also referred to ironically as competition of interest, we can also sense the temptation the security analyst must face every day in the exciting role of duty to an employer, which often times is a bank or mutual fund, and the companies about which they provide financial analysis. Further, the eager and sometimes young analysts were just happy to be a part of what makes the economy function. The only problem is that most of them see themselves as smart people who think 'think outside the box' is what needs to be done at all times and at any cost. This is their interpretation of what it means to perform, and most of them were looking to bring an entirely new way of looking at the economy to the table. Several securities analysts are 'young guns,' some fresh out of business school, who may not necessarily see their roles as sales adjuncts for bankers but rather see making their marks within the financial institutions in which they operate as a path toward an improved career (Stelzer, 2004) . They could only think of how 'stand out' performance could help get them noticed. For them, there was nothing wrong with pushing the envelope, and the attitude may have been, 'what could possibly go wrong?'

The shareholder, the third leg of the stool of human factor, in their own focus on performance, arguably did fall asleep at the switch. Clearly some people advocate shareholder primacy by making the claim that a company that focuses on profit will be an efficient and profitable one (Mangan, 2006). Before having to point out how unrelated these ideas are, it is worth playing devils advocate before we chastise the poor shareholder in the role of financial police. Perhaps the story of a man who charged the expenses for buying his wife handbags and throwing her a lavished birthday party is an easy target, that might be nothing more than a misbehavior that should be dealt with using appropriate company disciplinary policy procedures. That is not any more than a habitual generous tipper on a company trip who ends up tipping more than the percentage the company recommends and whose expense report was eventually adjusted by the superior, meaning he had to foot the rest of the difference. Saying that people lived lavished lifestyles does not explain corporate corruption. It, however, may explain the euphoria of good times when a rising tide lifted all boats, including the boats of shareholders who may have interpreted the seeming successes of the companies they have invested in as deserved results. Besides looking at the shareholders and institutional investors who had their own vested interest in profit, there was a culture that was being created, a culture where the rest of the population is living vicariously through the life of the rich and successful. Society rewarded them for their performances and gave them a reason to look at themselves as wealth creators for the rest of us (New Statesman, 2004). Perhaps it is the other way around. Perhaps the shareholders indeed hoped that the company executives were wealth creators, after all, they have a vested interest in the performance of the company. Either way, we cheered them on and one could argue that none of it started with greed, but rather with intent to see successful and high-performing companies in a vibrant economy. We could not blame culprits any more than the market system itself that is designed for intense performance and hence regulation. Further, there seems to be an unwillingness to trade good business ethics for big vibrant and thriving business (Risen, 2004). So, another way to look at how the market shapes the role of the shareholder is to say that being popular in school and being a nice guy are mutually exclusive. Often times, a school girl might opt for the adventure of going out with the wild and popular school boy even with the knowledge of a potential heartbreak, rather than go with the non exciting safer choice. As if to say that the thoughts of a high-flying executive should not be curtailed because it is holding ourselves back from bigger and better things, we seem to have left it to fate because as far as we are willing to know, only the dare devils can get things done and that such is the only urge that guaranteed success.

All this said, it is worth reminding ourselves that the theme of the Olympics is Citius, Altius, Fortius, which is Latin for 'Faster, Higher, Stronger.' The Olympic athlete is expected to perform, and he knows it. In fact, he wants it more than the people who expect it of him. For the Olympic athlete, it is about performance, first and foremost. It is arguably accurate to think of a corporation in the same way. It was the need to be bigger that drove businesses to monopolistic tendencies. Before the Great Depression, people and businesses knowingly or unknowingly charted a new territory with under consumption and over investment. The arrival of a new business theory that focuses on earnings management is necessitated by a business environment that is built on growth and innovation. Inevitably, the competitive nature of the capitalist market environment necessitates innovation and improvement that any company is required to demonstrate in order to stay ahead. It is hard to imagine a company that would set out hoping to perform worse than its prior year, as it would be hard to imagine that a company that is not under any pressure to best its prior year performances might find itself in corporate transgressions. There simply would be no motivation for it. So, evident in what we have seen is the thought that the pressure to perform on the part of business executives and securities analysts, and the demand for performance by institutional investors and shareholders alike, is the reason for corporate malfeasance that we have seen time and again.

The way we act, or the way we determine how to act, the way we answer the question, 'How should I act?' is driven by any value that we predetermine.

It is not a right or wrong proposition, but it is worth it to look at what drives us more so than to look at how we should act because any compelling, prevailing case we could make for possibilities, for the outcomes that we create, rests on a certain useful starting point. This useful starting point is whatever the value, or driver, is that we have defined.

Of course, the value that a person comes up with is just an idea of a certain weight. Precisely, it is the heaviest weight he can lift. If a money manager decides to use funds from people's pension to buy himself a nice house, then that is an idea that has a weight associated with it. The reason he spends other people's money is not because he is a good person or a bad person or a community leader or a religious person. The reason is that this is the best thought he can think.

As I have said, a person's goal in a situation is to avoid defects. A defect is anything that is contrary to what will become evident. A person avoids these defects by his ability to think the appropriate thought necessary to avoid the defect. Seeking that ability, creating a world where such a framework becomes our only preoccupation is the singular goal of the conversation that I am hoping that writing this book will introduce. If the idea to defraud people of their pension weighs 100 pounds and the thought of the consequences, on the household and communities and society as a whole, of a bunch of families losing their safety net weighs 150 pounds, or the thought of going to jail for eighteen years weighs 200 pounds, the money manager's options are clear. If not taking the people's money is what becomes evident, the money manager will not be able to think it. He is at 100 pounds. A person cannot lift a weight that he is not strong enough to lift. It is fine that a person is not able to lift a weight. We are all in such a condition at one time or another. The question that the axiom established in this book poses is, do we live in a world where there is a gymnasium in every corner of society or do we live in one where there are ice cream parlors? Six months removed from a situation, what are the chances that a person who was at a 100 pound strength will have moved up to 120 pounds, and 150 pounds, and beyond? This is the only condition for whether or not he continues to defraud people.

One day at work, an associate came to tell me that we were out of an item. Apparently, someone told her that we were out. Knowing that this was not first-hand information, I encouraged the individual to double check. In fact, I also came along, not because I did not trust that the person could complete the task, but because I knew that we had a better chance of finding the item with both of us looking for it. The point being that it would be costly indeed to spend money on an item that we had in the inventory.

As it turned out, we were not out of the item. In this event, I immediately saw a teachable moment for both myself and my coworker about making sure that we checked and rechecked things, supply inventories, business processes, or even basic tasks, for accuracy. As I explained the magnitude of this approach, and mindset, to the success of our operation, I was completely taken aback when the only contribution I could illicit from the associate was, "why are you always picking on me? How come you are never hard on other people as you are on me? It is not like I know where everything is, I am still fairly new here."

I did not know what to think or where to start with comments like these. This loss of words may have been because the task literally in front of me was a daunting one. Perhaps a knee jerk reaction would be to engage this individual in a baseless conversation about how I was not being for or against anyone. This was a conversation that could turn into whether I bought lunch for the staff only on days that certain people were scheduled. There would be no end to the sort of fabricated claims we could become tangled in.

This was not the choice I would want. I absolutely refused to have such a conversation, not because it would be a waste of my time, but solely because it would leave me not addressing with my associate what had to be done in the future to ensure that we did not spend money buying items that we had on the shelves. There was no way that I would let this associate get away from this conversation without acknowledging the glaring point that on the day when our operation was about to be constrained because of a failure to locate resources, this person wanted to talk about unicorns.

I should mention that this individual did not stay on our team for long, and I suppose the reason was that there was a characteristic elevation in the type of conversation that we were having as a team, one that the individual could not understand or be assimilated into. It was clear to my associate that we were not speaking the same language and that if there was a founded conversation to have about my disposition toward a staff member, I responsibly would not shy away from it. On this day, however, the conversation that we needed to have was about developing skills to navigate daily hotel operation, and acknowledging why a check and recheck culture fit into it.

I see similarities in this experience and what I observe sometimes especially on the political stage when I am listening to people from opposing campaigns and thinking, "I wonder how many people are listening to what these two people are saying and thinking, 'these two are actually not speaking the same language – not in the same room.'"

The words that come out of a person's mouth have to not only make sense, but they also have to be relevant. It eventually will no longer be socially acceptable to say something nonsensical. The more people are able to ponder what is possible on a level different in intensity or elevation than where we are collectively, the more guarantee we have of a different outcome.

When I went back to school after about a decade of abandoning my quest for higher education, I was like a kid in a candy store. There was simply this great union between life experiences that I had had up until that point, my love for ensuring that things were reasonably sorted out, and the knowledge that I was acquiring in my various courses. One thing that stuck out immediately in my mind in terms of application occurred when I started to do research papers. There were pieces of information that I needed to include with every annotation, and one of them is a description of why I had considered an author cited as credible. I started laughing. I thought it was funny learning this;

having my school tell me, "Don't think you can just tell us anything and expect us to believe it!" This is respect. This is serious. I got serious. My mind understood this responsibility immediately.

One day, a lady who sold advertisement blocks in a real estate magazine showed up at my hotel. She was very beautiful, and she was dressed provocatively. Do not get me wrong, her appearance was appropriate for a business environment, even when her ample chest area is assessed by such standards. However, when she snapped over and reached in her carrying case for a brochure, as she did many times, there was no missing the glorious sight that was her breasts.

Now, I could not say that she was sent to my office to tempt me, or that there was a correlation between someone as easy on the eye as she was and how many spaces her company ended up selling for the magazine. I could, however, say that I was in no fog about two things. The first thing was I was aware of the type of thoughts that I, like most, if not all, young, single, red blooded professional guys, could entertain. The second thing that was obvious to me was that the sales representative's appearance was of no interest to me. My interest was the cost and benefit of buying an advertisement in a real estate magazine. If I wanted to see an attractive lady with broad chest, there was a time for it, but not then. I knew that this was how I should act. It was obvious.

Perhaps the way we tend to describe things to ourselves using words like rational and irrational is how we try to admit to ourselves that we have problems that we are working out. That is, instead of the fear of thinking that we cannot be expected to be logical sometimes because we are not machines, I have to wonder if we have looked and interpreted our condition this way, bringing machines into the conversation, only to give ourselves an 'out' for times when we do appear to be so obviously intellectually incapable.

It is reasonable to expect that the closer we get to a useful starting point, the better we would be able to answer the question of how we should act. There is perhaps a framework for how we act with which we should concern ourselves. The outcomes that we create are based entirely on the paradigm that we can shift.

The idea of whether how we act is right or wrong is a nonentity.

If a logistics company that has a standard of seventy stops for its delivery drivers decided to change to eighty stops per day, it would not be the end of the world. Life would probably be more difficult for the driver because he had to do more, but the company might be focused less on that and more on how getting drivers to do more without increase in pay would increase profitability. A hotel company with hundreds of properties in its portfolio might wonder what getting every room attendant to clean rooms in fifteen minutes instead of twenty five would translate to in dollar amount.

There is an outcome that we could create that focuses on how incredible a company is, or one that speaks of an executive as an expert in turning companies around. We could use how much growth a company experiences in revenue and profit terms as a measure. We could establish how much money a company could make as a getting to the light moment. Of course, of the many ways a company could find itself growing, it could consider the cost of such growth as an outcome in itself.

This is not a reasoning that creates a path toward sympathy. No. We are not all going to get to the traffic light at the same time. This is acceptable. We should, however, not create an outcome that would cause any of us to say, "The reason a vehicle did not make it through the light was that another person was distracted with a phone conversation and as a result did not pick up the pace." This is on the one hand. On another hand, we could create an outcome that causes a person to say, "I knew I was not going to make it thought the light, but the person in front of me could have if we had all done our best to focus on getting as many vehicles through as we could."

We are not all going to be able to live a comfortable life where we are able to afford everything our hearts desire. I do not expect a company to hope that a housekeeper would make enough to be able to afford a plate of lobsters from time to time and a nice retirement account when it was all said and done. I do, however, think that not looking for a way to get a person to do in fifteen minutes a job that otherwise takes twenty-five minutes is a different outcome for how we could act.

THE BARACK OBAMA JUNCTURE

4 ON WHAT IS BEAUTIFUL

ON THE OUTSIDE

The reason we act the way we do is that we are not intelligent enough to act otherwise.

There is a good chance that what we currently think is beautiful may not be what we should consider as beautiful. Obviously, every single thing that we have to figure out requires using our mind to do so. As a result, this becomes a game of outcomes, depending on the mind's fitness level. For starters, we may decide not to use our mind. This is most evident in the idea of stereotype. In this phenomenon, a person may decide to look at another person a certain way, or he may have predetermined how he sees another person. This is not because he has discovered how that person truly is but because he has decided that true discernment might require too much effort. So, he resorts to shortcuts, making stuff up, when the real work of perceiving and interpreting what is going on is too burdensome for him. Whether we use our mind or not, there is an outcome that we create, there is a world that we paint. The world that we create is the only thing that is worth contemplating in the sense of what is beautiful. In other words, we should be compelled to ask if the world we are creating is really beautiful or not.

As a matter of a useful starting point, a person may think that something is beautiful only because his mind does not want to do the work of finding what actually is beautiful. So, it is quite possible that what is beautiful is not how magnificent a house is but rather how closely the inhabitants live together. Of course, it is easier to design a marvel of a building than to work to live in a useful way inside that house. It is quite possible that what is beautiful is not how much a person has managed to collect in art work, but what fulfillment he derives when he invites people over for dinner around his table and they each give him a hug and a kiss on their way home. But then, it probably costs less to collect paintings than it does to develop what could become a priceless hug from a person.

What is beautiful is the world that we are able to create. What is beautiful is the outcome of the ideas that lurk in our minds. Up until now, this ability, this imagination, this longing, for something majestic, something magnificent, is something that we have inadequately portrayed or misrepresented as art, in the form of painting, or music, or poetry, or sculpture. Granted, we should marvel at such creations. However, that which is fine, that which is excellent, that which is costly, and rare, and difficult to attain, is not anything that can be destroyed or that changes from day to day or that can be subjected to different view points. What is beautiful, the reflection that we have hoped would satisfy the senses and emotions that we have, is not in art or nature, or any object that we have created, or that we can create. The conditions or outcomes that our mind is capable of fashioning are what make something beautiful.

What we want to be able to describe as beautiful, and artistic, and breath taking, is not what the mind has worked toward for its satisfaction. We are at a disadvantage in this regard because the reason we act the way we do is that we are not intelligent enough to act otherwise. So, here we are, separated yet again; this time from what we think is beautiful and what we would find actually is. What the mind is working toward, its struggle for what brings it pleasure and satisfaction, I suspect, is not a collection of shoes, or an exotic automobile, or glitters around the neck, or even music that takes the mind to a different place. Nevertheless, these are all wonderful things, and it would not be the end of the world to have considered them the meaning or focus of aesthetics.

I would not be able to build consensus on the worth of a painting, or that of a piece of jewelry. I might not even be able to guarantee my own emotional satisfaction for such, a day or two removed. I might not be able to get a person thousands of miles away on the other side of the world to see eye to eye with me on what makes a car to which I am enthralled so beautiful. I suspect that the reason for this is that these are not what the mind is seeking to cure its longing or fill its void for what it considers beautiful. The reason for this is that what is beautiful is something that costs the mind to see, or to attain, or to accomplish.

It is possible that the way we have attempted to define what is beautiful generally, and synonymously philosophically, is really a trial on our way to exactly what it is that we are trying to achieve, what it is that we are trying to express. This condition is not unlike one where a special needs kid with a clear picture in his mind begins to communicate that picture to his parents. Of course, because language is a barrier, a veil, a foggy screen, an obstacle, it takes a while for his parents to succeed in properly recreating in their own minds the picture that the kid is trying to communicate, which is the picture that he sees in his mind.

Finding a satisfactory answer to the question of what is beautiful is a matter of a useful starting point. We could consider that it is a person with a white skin or a person with a black skin that makes for what is beautiful. We could say that the criterion for human beauty is height. We could just come out and say it: a tall person clears the beauty bar, and a short person does not. Alternatively, maybe it is how well sculpted a person's body is that makes him beautiful, and the teddy bear types should just 'stay home.' Could it really be what a person looks like that makes him beautiful?

Besides the fact of the subjective nature of this way of looking at beauty whereby a person could dismissively tell us what he found beautiful, what would a person have to say for himself if five years after he swore, for instance, that only tall people were beautiful, he found himself looking at short people in a different light? Better yet, what are the chances that a person who considered another person beautiful might, one-day look at such a person and not find him beautiful anymore?

At my job, what is beautiful to me is not the building architecture. It is not the lobby design, or the compelling artwork that you see as you step out of the elevator landing that makes our hotel beautiful. It is not the oversized rooms or the giant size television that makes for unique room appointment. What is beautiful is how much closer, given the challenges of the day, including human differences that we have to bridge, we can get to the cleanest product and the best service. This is the world that we intend to create. We could try to say that it is how physically attractive the people who work behind the front desk are. We could pretend that it is the thread count of towels in our bathrooms that is beautiful. We could focus on the material nature of things. We could work day and night to make this the world that we could create at the hotel. We could believe this to be what was beautiful. If we did, it would not be the end of the world only we would not know what else is possible.

Years ago, I wrote an article that was inspired by the time I had devoted to finding ways to improve our business operation. I titled the article: Methods for Excellence in Business Operations. At the time, my thinking was that it benefited a business if front line associates were as knowledgeable as 'executives' in the business operation of which they were a part. More radically, I thought it would not be acceptable for any associate to want to just do his job and go home, never questioning how his job connected with those of others. My instincts were such that the associate of a company viewed himself as responsible in the decision making for the company as much as the Chief Executive Officer did. And in such a company, because everyone was trained like the CEO, a line level employee did not wait until he was paid like the CEO to put the necessary effort into wanting to learn everything that he possibly could about the hotel business. Therefore, I thought that if the front line is seen as the lifeline, the most advanced training, and the most time devoted to training, would be happening at the front line.

In any case, here is the article that I wrote at the time. I wanted to share it to see if what I was thinking at the time still falls in line with my thinking today. I also wanted to see if it had any application for the philosophies that I espouse, given that I see the workplace as a microcosm of the world. I also wanted to see if there are any lessons to deduce for this section of the book.

For those of us who operate a business, there are so many areas in which we are required to achieve excellence in order to deliver superior product and service, and we know what a daunting task it is in terms of what it takes to bring success about. Most of us would acknowledge that operating philosophy is what separates one company from another, one business from the competitor around the corner. However, in an ever-changing business world, more and more of us are restless looking at operating philosophy the same way that we did for decades when guiding principles were formed at the top and instructions, often in the form of job descriptions and checklists, were passed down the operating ladder.

I suspect that a new way of thinking is on the horizon, one in which operating philosophy is viewed only as an aggregate of high-minded operating level methods.

The philosophy of method brings greater focus to what goes on at the frontline of a business operation by reversing the role and regarding the frontline as the boardroom, thereby requiring the frontline associate to be more than executors of the new and revised corporate instructions. The expectation that the method required to deliver superior product and service is not one thought out at the top and then delivered to the frontline but rather developed on the frontline itself brings a different dimension to business operation and business success. Ultimately, competitive advantage could be realized not just in how much time is devoted to training but particularly in whether there is method beyond a training guide or a job checklist.

In order words, if we asked of business operators how many would expect their associates to operate based on nothing more than the instructions that were handed down to them, I suspect consensus would be that more was required.

Consider a hotel housekeeping associate who regularly failed to turn in 'perfect' rooms. We might expect that turning in exceptionally clean rooms was a daily hurdle that the housekeeping staff had to clear. We would find that a person could clean a room up nicely but still end up leaving something in the room that did not belong. And often, the effort of a near 'perfect' room was marred by easily corrected errors. How did this happen time and time again, a dry cleaner hanger, water in the iron, alarm clock that was set by the previous occupant? Why did it sometimes require the housekeeping inspector or supervisor to find and correct these errors and not the person who spent thirty minutes cleaning the room?

In light of the failure in the face of training and re-training, it is easy to grow increasingly reluctant to the role that training plays. Telling the housekeeping staff what went in a room and what did not, plastering the 'cleaning cycle' all over the employee break room and making every housekeeper memorize and recite it on a whim, might not be the answer to getting people to be competent at what they did. Instead, one might expect that what was missing is a consciousness, an interaction, a bond, between a housekeeper and her room. I am convinced that a high mind on the frontline is as important as any high-minded approach that could originate from the boardroom, or at the top of the organizational structure.

In my experience, what I was able to do was to convince my housekeeping staff that the reason they cleaned was not to make a room clean but rather to give the person who rented the room the unequivocal impression that she was the first person to ever set foot in that room. There was a sixth sense about the process that went beyond carrying out job duties. It was a sense that called every action to life by acknowledging that what any person did, if done well, was equally as important and complex as what any other person did; from the top of an organization to the bottom. Quite possibly, the person on the front line has as many, perhaps more complex, dots to connect as anyone else in an organization. I am not sure if we have looked at this outcome.

The approach allowed the housekeeper to see her job as an interaction between a person and a room. It created a reason for the thought, 'There is something organic in what I am about to do in this room, something alive.' This quickly turned into an exercise which purpose was to send a message to the guest who rented the room, an exercise that compelled the housekeeper to go further than cleaning and straightening up. For instance, with the mindset, a housekeeper would not only ensure that a lamp shade was not crooked but also that it looked fresh and new. The housekeeper with this needed broad sense could make calls like changing out stained ironing board covers, or making notes for the maintenance department to remove scuff marks on room walls.

In a dynamic environment such as a hotel operation, it is impossible to list every scenario for a housekeeper of what to expect in a room that has been vacated. I am not sure there is enough time for such training. In my opinion, the preoccupation to give instructions in an endlessly exhaustive manner is looking more like an obsolete attempt to spoon-feed operating level associates. Perhaps the approach accomplishes much but in no way compares to an approach where the focus is to require associates to see the job duty as only a means to an end; an approach that looks beyond understanding job duties.

For companies that think there is importance to applying strong principles that determine overall health of the company, principles that brand the company and separate it from its competitors, there may be another frontier out there. There may be a frontier where it is more important to apply high mind at the bottom with the expectation that there is a better result when <u>philosophy in method</u> is introduced on the frontline rather than in the boardroom.

In a way that now we see more and more companies adopt a culture that empowers the associates on the frontline, in contrast to years ago when such service culture was more of the exception, the constantly evolving business environment might find its future operating models and successes not in associates who prefer to be told what to do but rather in those who are able to synthesize their actions and efforts with the overall health of the business.

We are the ones who created the world that we live in. We did this, in part, because we asked ourselves the question, 'what is beautiful?' We had an urge for this. Of course, this is a question that begets other questions. For instance, could we say that what is beautiful is an employee on the front line who believes that his role is as important as that of everyone else in the company? Could we say that this is what is beautiful? And would we say this only because it creates a world more useful than the alternative? Or should we just leave this whole idea of beauty to what a person feels as long as he can separate himself as a person from others by his status or material wealth?

What is beautiful is not the words that a person uses; it is the ideas that he is trying to convey. On the one hand, a person could think that what obtains are his strategies, and the words that he has tested for the best response from the people he engages. On the other hand, a person might be convinced that it is his ideas that will prevail. Still in this, we have to determine what is beautiful. That is, either way, there is a world that we create, one that is blinded by a veil and one that is not.

The people I work with are encouraged that our focus is not that we are proficient with the tools that we use to run our business. There is a way to see what we do through this lens and consequently, there is a hotel that we create as a result of this outlook. We could work harder every day trying to learn how to get from one screen to the other, from one module to another. However, this is not how we have approached our business. We do not want our effort to be cosmetic. The world we try to create is one where we have imagined what would happen if those tools – those computers – that we use to run the hotel were taken away. This approach has worked well for us. We do not panic when the printer does not work or when the computers crash. This does not bother us at all because we know that the reason we do what we do is not because we have fast computers or intelligent applications. We have seen what we do beyond those computers that we use. Our understanding of what we do is independent of the computers that we use as tools.

There are many examples that we could come up with to explain the world that we have created and the one that is possible.

One day, I was at Outback Steakhouse having lunch. On the television was an incredible tennis match between Jo-Wilfried Tsonga and tennis legend Roger Federer. As I watched this match, where one player with odds against him, gave the best that he had in order to win a match against a formidable opponent, it was so obvious what it cost to be able to do such a thing - the desire, the belief, the passion, the pain, the doubts. It was quite evident in this match what it cost to be extraordinary. There was no doubt in my mind that sport stars are famous because we are all drawn to the sense, to the witness, of what is possible, of what is extraordinary.

After lunch, I went to Starbucks to do some work. There, I met a lady who was studying for a medical examination. We chatted awhile. From talking to her, I discovered the difficulty of her task at hand. I could tell that she had a formidable opponent. I started to prod her because I wanted to analogize her endeavor with what I had just witnessed in the tennis match. Though her condition was controlled differently, I wanted to know if she was feeling the adrenalin, or if she would feel it on the day of her certification examination. I wanted to know if she brought the same 'game' to her study, or if she was going to on the day of the examination. I wanted to see how maddening it was to do what she committed herself to do.

Really though, I wanted to imagine if the whole world could look at her on the day of that medical examination the same way that we do when we watch a match like the one between Jo-Wilfried Tsonga and Roger Federer. I wanted to wonder if we could make her famous the same way that we have made Tsonga and Federer famous.

ON THE INSIDE

The only struggle we are in is the one with our minds, each of us, individually, with no one else involved.

The position that we should consider other possibilities with regards to what we think is beautiful brings me to a second thought that in itself could be looked at as what is beautiful. This second thought poses the question. 'Can the mind confront itself?'

I drank a lot at one point in my life. I think it is safe to say that I drank very heavily. I do not believe that personal hardships and regrets and failures at the time were directly linked to the way that I abused alcohol, or that they might have had any correlation with the downward progression of my emotional state. What is clear is that I drank a lot, including hard liquor, every day. Over the course of a few years, the changes that I was going through in real life, like career changes and normal feelings about self-actualization, were exacerbated by the inevitable damage that drinking was doing to any clarity that I could exercise.

At some point, all this became a study for me. There were days that I thought that my life was worth nothing, and I should kill myself. I even observed that I only had this thought, on most days, in the morning hours. Often, as the day progressed, I would begin to gain control of my thoughts. I mean that I would have an easier time looking at my situation, and this often meant that I began to have better thoughts. For instance, I would be able to think that things were not as bad as I thought, and that I would be okay. I even began to notice that my emotional state on these mornings might have depended on what type of drink I had the night before and how much I had to drink; for example, dark liquor or a mixture.

It was ugly. I knew during these times that I was creating a different life and a different world for myself, and probably for people around me. At the same time that I had this very dark life, my mind was still capable of knowing that I could choose to create a different reality. Whatever my woe-is-me story was, or that my mind could be deceiving me into thinking existed, I knew for one thing that I did not want to kill myself per chance that things were not as bad as I saw them. I just knew that this would be poor judgment. Somehow, it was evident to me that at any one point, what I was feeling might not have been an accurate reflection of my condition. My mind was busy, but I knew I could still use it to separate my realities. I could use my mind to tell my mind that even though it was feeling down, I should give it a couple of hours. I simply endured.

It was painful to have to deal with what I could safely describe as serious chemical imbalance. It actually hurt. I did not have a clear mind, aggregately. As a result, my overall personality was changing, not that I could substantiate a link to my drinking. The one that makes me laugh the most was on most days, I thought that I was going to lose my job. However, on other days, I clearly saw the path to reinvention. I saw that in a matter of a couple of years, I could completely find myself in a different place.

So when I found myself pursuing a degree and writing a book, though I struggled, it was clear to me that I had better things to do than drink. I found that I needed my mind, but my mind was not capable of doing these things that were more important to me. This was a very important lesson for me because I knew the sort of world that I was creating as a result of my drinking. I knew the world I was creating after a public episode at a local restaurant and what that meant to my girlfriend at the time. I knew that this had nothing to do with how well-dressed or how handsome I looked that night. It had nothing to do with valeting my sports car. What I was creating was not beautiful.

From my experience, I knew that what I could consider beautiful is this place that I could go, this world that I could create, one that had no resemblance to anything that is seen as beautiful in the traditional sense. Even a beautiful sunset may not look beautiful some days. I pondered a world that we would be creating if we all ran around half drunk most of the time. I considered the sort of outcome that we would be painting when the average college graduate only sees the world through the lens of addiction to prescription medication.

What to qualify as beautiful is the sort of outcomes that we are able to create with the mind that we have. This could be a reality that is created by addiction to prescription medication, or it could be one where we have valued a clear mind.

Early on when I started to write, when I started to notice what my mind could think and how it wanted to express these thoughts with words, it was natural for me to wonder what more my mind could do if it were altered. Obviously, this is not some spectacular thought. It is possible that influence or societal standards were what caused me to think that my mind would be 'better' or able to do more, or become more creative, or imagine better, if I had stimulated it with, say, drugs and alcohol.

Of course now, I am convinced that the mind could do all that on its own. The point to make is not at all that I should leave my mind alone but rather that I at least know the choice between when my mind is without the influence of stimulants and when it is and which one I should pursue, and when. I find that this is a beautiful thing to know. I find that it is beautiful for me to know what it has cost me to come to this conclusion. There is a distinction between the world that we have used shortcuts to create and one that has come about through clearheaded birthing.

What is beautiful is rare and difficult for the mind to attain. For this reason, the mind will not attain what is beautiful, it cannot attain it, except on its own and without aid. A man cannot attain what is beautiful by having it fed to him. The only struggle we are in is the one with our minds, each of us, individually, with no one else involved.

The possibility that I am trying to create can be explained by two worlds. In the one world, a person goes through four years of college essentially by relying on other students to do the work for him. In the other world, a student confronts himself and embodies the knowledge that the courses he is required to take are meant to impart. On the one hand, you could let your friends write your papers for you and do your assignments for you because you find it inconvenient to dive into the subject matter. It could be required to endure and to master and to do what it takes to study and read materials again and again and again, and to take days to understand what a term means. There is a world that is created as a result of you becoming that. This is what is beautiful – not a house, not a car.

What kind of world is a person creating after having gone to a soccer match where he spent his time not watching the game but hurling insults and vitriolic remarks at players on the field? What appeal will he create after he has spent his time calling players monkeys, throwing banana peels on the pitch, and

making jungle noises in order to insult? Could this person get home, being capable of these thoughts, then draw a masterpiece or create an impeccable architecture and by so doing make the world beautiful?

In similar light, a man who batters his wife may find that this is not beautiful – particularly if his wife prefers that she is not bloodied from time to time. This man will have a choice in creating a world where he is compelled to think that the way to get his wife not to look at another man is not to keep her locked up in the house or follow her around when she goes out. In a sense, we should wonder – since the question that we have posed to ourselves, the question that we are attempting to answer, is on what is beautiful – if the vehicle that a man who abuses his wife drives is what is beautiful to him, or to his wife, or to his neighbors, or to the world. We should wonder if it is how tall he is or the color of his skin or is athletic physique or the buildings that he has helped design or the things he has painted in his spare time that he has loaned to the local art gallery what to consider beautiful.

What is beautiful is what the mind can imagine even though it lives in an environment where the only television stations you see are those controlled by your government. **In other words, what is beautiful is what the mind can do to see beyond the veil, the obstacle, the foggy screen, that is between him and that which is possible.**

What is beautiful is not what we look at and think is beautiful. What is beautiful is what brings us closer to what is, what is true, what is permanent.

At work one day, I caught myself in the middle of a situation thinking, "There is a good chance that the reason I am acting this way right now is because I am hungry." It was funny. It was an epiphany. It was an experience that I have used to train myself, and those with whom I work. On that day, I caught myself in the middle of the world that I was creating, acknowledging that the reason I reacted to a situation the way I did was because I was hungry. I thought that this lesson was important enough for me in that I could suddenly imagine a world where the reason everything occurred was because some dude was hungry. This could not possibly be something beautiful. It could not possibly be a beautiful thing to set my staff off, making a bad day of it for them, for the world that they were capable of creating that day, all because I was hungry.

It is not just that I recognize this; it also is that a colleague is aware that if he is addressed in a certain way, before burning down the house, it is okay to wonder if Christian is hungry. This is the world that we can elect to create. This is what is beautiful for us at the end of the day; that we have not gone over some deep end caused by a chain reaction that started because somebody was hungry.

I was watching Stephen Colbert one night, and his guest was Dr. Nassir Ghaemi. In his book, A First-Rate Madness: Uncovering the Links Between Leadership and Mental Illness, Dr. Ghaemi takes the position that mental illness can be useful for great leadership.[16] Dr. Ghaemi makes the case that there are mood disorders that can cause a person to have different types of thoughts, including some that may end up being creative. This is an interesting observation on Dr. Ghaemi's part in thinking that a person with mental illness might have certain advantages that a normal person might not have. I would consider this point only to compare it to the fascination that a girl might have for the guy on campus who everyone considers interesting, but the reason he is interesting and confident and creative and witty is because he is on drugs. The girl would have her ups with the guy, but she is also going to have her serious downs with him as well.

My point is, if the price of admission now is that we have to be a little crazy then there is a world that we create with that. If what a person wants to think is that he drives really well after a few drinks, or that he becomes slightly more focused, should we afford him that? Should we resign ourselves to the thought that the only way that a person can be compelling is by being slightly unhinged? Is the world that we prefer to create one with a bunch of slightly unhinged people? And if it turns out that with a little work, a normal mind, by itself, could attain creativity and ambition and genius, which would we prefer? Which of these two worlds would we be prepared to be a part of, one with a brilliant, maddening, and unpredictable individual or one with a brilliant, maddening, and predictable individual?

I am saying all these things so that we can begin a dialogue because a person's purpose is not to become a doctor or a lawyer or a supreme court justice or a garbage collector. A person's purpose is to avoid defects. If we find out that what we thought was beautiful all along is not what is beautiful, that would not be beautiful, that would be a defect. To avoid defects a person must improve his logic – his ability to think a valid thought. Of course, the ability to think a valid thought, a thought that is appropriate for what will become evident, is not something any of us can come by easily.

Beyond objects, what is beautiful are the conditions that the mind is able to create. What is beautiful is the commitment that we could make to pursue what works.

One day I was talking to a man who, among other things, was a retired pilot. We were talking about processes, business processes to be exact. He shared with me that long after he retired from flying he was on a flight and it was time to start serving meals. The passenger sitting next to him had ordered a cup of coffee and as he was being served, the retired pilot noticed that the flight attendant first placed the coffee cup on the food tray in the passenger's lap and then she brought the coffee decanter to it – to the cup. Of course, a small turbulence and some coffee spill later, the poor passenger needed a change of clothes. I got excited listening to my friend. I told him that I had a similar story whereby I told a person who was about to clean a surface to spray the rag and not the surface.

There is work in the mind that goes into arriving at business processes that work. The world that we create as a result of this labor is what I consider beautiful – and not necessarily an approach that proves to work but rather the everyday intent to pursue the idea of what works. The coffee decanter is not what is beautiful, but how we use it can be. We could elect to think that the coffee decanter was what is beautiful, or we could acknowledge that how we end up using it might be the satisfaction that our need for art seeks. In the word of dear Mr. Michael Franks, there is a reason every blossom turns toward the sun.[17]

So, we are faced with the choice of looking at beauty as something present, or immediate, or even superficial. The other option is a bit involved. The other option is work because it requires us to connect, or feel, or be involved. A friend and I were talking about music the other day. She is a music student, and we were talking about her grades. I was interested in how an instructor would go about grading the work of a music student. We talked about what I thought was an enormous burden for the instructor in coming up with the standards to use in assessing the work of a student of the Arts. On a non academic level, I thought that a teacher had a daunting task of knowing where a student is coming from with her work and that the beauty is revealed only after a level of familiarity.

Interestingly, during our conversation, I recalled my own unique experience as someone who listens to music extensively, and with great devotion. Specifically, I acknowledged that many years ago, I did not find jazz appealing at all. In fact, when I bought my first jazz music, it was a cassette of Earl Klugh's Tropical Legs, and I could only listen to one track. There was only one track on that cassette that I could tolerate, or enjoy, or digest. After a while, however, often times by accidentally leaving tracks playing, my ears began to 'open up.' I remember the day that I realized I was not just able to listen to every single track on the album, I was enjoying them.

There is probably a strong case to make for my journey from when I could only manage to listen to one track to how I now look forward to listening to every song. There was a level of familiarity that started to develop between myself and the tracks on my Earl Klugh cassette, one that is perhaps one and the same with the story that was developing, the story that started when I bought my Earl Klugh cassette. The story that is built with parts like the day I ran into someone who talked about what a great jazz musician Mr. Klugh is. The story that continued when a friend mentioned that there was a jazz concert, and I reluctantly obliged to an invitation, and was fed a good dose of the music that is jazz.

So, on the one hand, what we think is beautiful, for all practical purposes, is superficial. It is the sort of beauty interpretation that we find ourselves wanting to make when we see a woman who is attractive with a man who is not so attractive and we just would like to say, "How did he get such a beautiful woman?" And it is possible in many cases that a woman might even admit that left alone to physical appearance, that a person stood no chance. The story that is often told in this type of cases points to how a person appears more beautiful as familiarity grows and other character traits are revealed. Conversely, we might not find a person as beautiful as we once accepted the person to be, maybe after experiencing multiple verbal or physical abuse from the person, or after watching the person get intoxicated and act in unattractive ways.

The other level of beauty to ponder, consequently, is one that seems to transcend what is superficial, one that seems conceptual, one that seems to appeal to our complete sense rather than just that of sight or hearing or touch or smell or even taste. Put differently, there is a chance that we are able to look at what is beautiful in a completely different light. Only getting to that point will require tremendous work on the part of the mind.

One time on a trip to New York City, I drove around and thought how cool it must be to live in New York City. I could tell how proud the people who lived there were. I got the sense that their energy, or swagger, was in knowing that they played host to so many visitors from all over the world. This had to be an incredible state of mind in itself. More so, I thought how nice it must be to have an apartment in one of those high rises that are known to be expensive. And then I thought that if I were someone who really enjoyed that life and saw it as an important value, to what extent would I go to keep it. What would I do in order to keep my job, say, at a television station, so that I could keep my lifestyle? Would I say things on television not because I believed what I was saying, but because I got paid to say them?

At my job, I go to great length to encourage the people with whom I work not to say things that are unfounded because I know that this will set us back. A submarine might run aground if it is fed inaccurate information by its sonar system. Every time we falsely say things to one another, our operation would suffer. This outweighs everything. It outweighs our personalities, our quirks, our dysfunctions. I prefer a world where we can deliver in spite of those things. This is what to consider beautiful.

THE BARACK OBAMA JUNCTURE

5 ON WHAT IS BEYOND

The reason we act the way we do is that we are not intelligent enough to act otherwise.

I have written this book because I wanted to create consensus on the thought that the way we act at any one time is the best way that we can act. A person who accidentally shuts the door behind himself while trying to sit a bag of trash outside as he makes dinner may have to call a neighbor, or a locksmith, or break a window, if he does not know how to jimmy the door open. A crime investigation will unfold one way or the other based on the limits of how those involved in the investigation can deconstruct the act.

Further, I have thought that our actions create outcomes, outcomes that become what the world looks like. If the person who locked himself out could not get back into the house early enough, he would run the risk of burning his dinner and setting his kitchen on fire and not going to work the next day because the insurance fellow had to appraise the damage. Likewise, the outcome of how a crime scene is acted upon could be that an innocent person ends up in prison, and a perpetrator gets to live to commit additional crimes.

Even further, I have thought that the way we act can change based on changes to what we know. This progression is the reason I have concluded that we really should only care about knowing more 'stuff.' In other words, I have thought that the result – a man setting his kitchen on fire because he did not have in his disposal the knowledge of an almost effortless way of getting back into his house, or an obvious oversight that sent an innocent man to prison – should not be a focus for us. The results should not be what we talk about. Rather, how to know more should be what we talk about because this will take care of the results. That is, the results will continue to change the more we know.

As it turns out, it appears that we are inclined to want to know, and hence, to want to know more. In the most fundamental way, this is evident in the experiences that our senses afford us and how we delight in them.

Take the sense of sight, for instance. I think it is delightful that we can see. This is so obvious because often, if not always, when we hear something, we naturally react to want to see it. At one time or another, we have demonstrated our appreciation for our ability to see, and hear, and smell, and taste, and feel.

Not long ago I was in traffic and for whatever reason I started to think how amusing, and important at the same time, it is that I have peripheral vision. For a minute, I was actually thinking what a disaster it would be on the road if I, and everyone else, did not have peripheral vision.

It is great that we are inclined to learning. This ability, however, exposes us to two realities. The first is that we could decide not to learn. The other is that we run the risk of learning things that are 'not there.' And there is a good chance that we may have done this already. We have ventured way out that every single one of us now has something to say about the questions that consume us, about our perennial gripping problems. Here are some of the questions that we ask: Does man have a soul? Is it possible that reality is just a construct of the mind? What is the meaning of life? These questions have only led to, and rightfully so, anyone of us being able to create his own doctrine.

Of course, if the goal we set out to achieve is to answer perennial gripping questions, it is highly unlikely that our best chance would be by any one of us making up his answers. I do not suspect that we would make advancement in unraveling the nature of what is, or of being, with this seeming freedom that we have to create our individual theories of what we think we are, or who we think we are, or if there is more to any of us than meets the eye.

Interestingly, I acknowledge that any effort that I make to state my view in itself undoubtedly amounts to my own doctrine on the matter of what it means to exist or what it is to be conscious, or any other questions of the sort worth asking. I recognize nonetheless that I may not have a choice. An analogy that comes to mind to explain this condition is that a person who would like another person to be quiet may have to verbalize his desire, there by violating what it is to be quiet. Another analogy that comes to mind is that in order to convince a group of people who may have thought that there was a destination that there was not one, one may actually have to travel somewhere.

In any case, before I make my doctrine known, I must attempt to find common ground on the challenge that language presents. Fundamentally, I would hope that instead of the tool that we use to communicate becoming a source, if not the source, of our inability to reason, that we would find as our most original metaphysical triumph a way to communicate without our thoughts getting lost in translation.

I was on the phone with a software vendor not long ago. We had considered changing our Property Management System, and this company was giving us a demonstration of their application in a web conference format. At one point, as I continued to drill in on the capability of the accounting module, I realized that we, both parties, were getting bogged down and confused in our usage of words and accounting jargon. So, in a way that I did not have to use the words 'statement' and 'invoice' and 'folio' at all, I described what I hoped that their system could do. At this point, instead of our presenter saying, "That is a matter of semantics," which was the phrase he had used multiple times in the presentation, he ended up saying, "No. Our system cannot do that."

In a way, I have discussed that at any one time, our struggle remains bridging the gap between what we think and what actually is, or that there is a veil, or an obstacle, or a foggy screen that stands between us and whatever it is that we have to see. I maintain that language itself can be one such veil, obstacle, or foggy screen. As a result, it is an exercise of the utmost order to be aware of this limitation.

If it turns out that one of the doctrines on metaphysics is correct, would it have anything to do with us? In other words, what are the chances that we could wake up one day to realize, after finally figuring out the nature of reality, that we would have to start doing things completely differently than we had been doing them? Could it turn out that this revelation would have no part in anything that we already knew, anything that we were?

Put differently, we would not learn anything about anything that is worth knowing from the outside in. We would not learn anything about the things that puzzle us in a way that such discovery would contradict our nature.

If a person concluded that reality is what happens when he is dreaming or that what we know now about anything is really a dream, we would probably say, "Sure, have at it." If another person thought that for everything that we know to exist, there is a bodiless form of that thing that does not perish, we would say, "Have fun thinking that." If yet another person held dear to the doctrine that there is no need to fuss over an imperishable form that nobody knows where it is and what it looks like, but that it is the things that have substance that comes first, we might say, "Here comes another one."

And literally, here comes another one because I also have an idea of what we should think of metaphysics. I have my own definition of what we think about ourselves and about today and about tomorrow and about the nature of things and about what is beyond everything that we know. There are two ways in which I have categorized my thought. For every thought that we entertain, or perhaps every act, there is what is useful or permanent, and there is what we could consider belief.

Metaphysics is the exercise that determines if a particular condition – a thought, a policy, a viewpoint, an act, and so on – is useful or permanent.

Our exercise in metaphysics is of utmost importance only in the sense that we could decide to engage in thoughts that would benefit us, or we could run the risk of thinking thoughts that not only may not be useful, but may be 'out there,' or farfetched. My point is that our metaphysical test is in whether anything that we have thought is useful in the first place. **This is what I consider to be philosophy.** THIS IS FIRST.

It is not enough for a person to say, "Here. This is what I am thinking." It is more important for that person to say, "This is what I am thinking, and it is permanent."

There is nothing that says that this is not made up stuff – the sort of thing that I am trying to avoid. By the time we go from one guy who thinks that the objects that we acknowledge are not the real deal but rather corresponding Forms that are immutable, to another guy who says that we should pay attention to the objects and that the objects can be traced back to the Unmoved Mover; we, again, are right in that territory where any one of us could come forward and state his case.

In a sense, our world itself could be like the one where an athlete who is bent on finding ways to excel is tempted to violate regulatory constraints placed on his sport. He might engage in acts that would constitute cheating. That is, an attempt to answer the question of what is 'out there,' or what is beyond, or the nature of things, is like the pursuits of an Olympic Drug Testing Body and that of an athlete who is interested in finding drugs that could help him jump higher, or lift stronger, or run faster; a drug that could not be detected in a test. As a result, there is an ever expanding world that the dynamic - the one between a regulatory body and any entity that is bent on outsmarting it - creates; a world that otherwise would not be there. Nothing is there yet until the athlete comes up with a performance-enhancing drug that is not yet on the banned substance list. Then the regulatory body catches up and puts it on the list. And the cycle is repeated, or essentially, the reality expands.

In a similar manner, a person with enough knowledge and whose focus is to continue to create new designer drugs for recreation beyond any sort of existing regulation will presumably have endless possibility to the extent to which he decides the reality or the nature of life for those who are in the business of regulating designer drugs.

One of the things that I remember about the story of a man who was shot dead because he would not stop eating the face of another man is not just that he was under the influence of a drug by the street name bathsalt, but also that the drug was not under any regulation or ban because it was new. Apparently, if you were, for instance, a chemical engineer who was out of a job and in need of a means of livelihood, you could use your knowledge to design drugs to sell to people who used drugs recreationally. At any time, you could design drugs that no regulatory body interested in banning drugs had thought ahead to ban. The challenge for those whose job it is to categorize what gets banned is really how many chemical compounds they are going to be able to round up and put on the list.

So, at the very least, whatever is out there, whatever is possible for us to discover, does not exist independent of our own validity. More importantly, it is worth saying that, in fact, it is our validity that determines the nature and scope of what is out there. So if there is anything metaphysical at all, anything worth considering that could be 'after' what is us, what is implicitly physical, it would have to involve us.

My point is that our challenge is in knowing that there is more relevance in figuring out what is within reach than what is beyond because if there is something beyond, it is highly unlikely that it exists to invalidate what is not beyond. It is more useful to think that we are a reduction or microcosm, if there is such a thing. Either way, our preoccupation should remain us. This is the only metaphysical pursuit that counts.

The only useful angle to our outlook on the metaphysical questions that we would like to answer simply is to pursue what is permanent. I have not used this word in the sense of what is universal or in terms of 'forms.' I have used this word knowing that thought will not be limited by language. I mean this in terms of the difference between what is certain to change, and what prevails.

So, instead of actually looking for what is after the physical, our idea of what is beyond, or what it means to exist, or what is real, is in front of us. If you had a person who wondered about having peripheral vision, it would be less useful for him to dwell on how he got his peripheral vision than it would be for him to learn to use it well.

My point is that what is metaphysical for us in a sense is not beyond but within.

THE QUESTION WE SHOULD BE ASKING IS NOT ONE OF WHAT IS A BEING BUT RATHER ONE OF WHAT IS PERMANENT. IN SAYING THIS, I HAVE PROVEN MY POINT FOR HOW TO DEFINE WHAT IS METAPHYSICAL. IN BEING, WE ARE ALL FREE TO EXERCISE ANY DOCTRINE AS WE ALLOW OUR STUDIES TO LEAD US. AS SUCH, IN CONSIDERING THAT WHAT IS PERMANENT IS THE MORE APPROPRIATE NOTION TO PONDER, I HAVE EXERCISED MY OWN DOCTRINE. HOWEVER, TO EXERMINE WHICH DOCTRINE WOULD NOT CHANGE ESTABLISHES A NEW ORIENTATION.

I could say that what is metaphysical is that we sped up when the light turned yellow as opposed to that we slowed down. We could make a big deal out of this. Of course, another person might say that it makes perfect sense to speed up when the light turns yellow. Another person might take the position that whether you speed up or slow down as you approach a traffic light that is changing should depend on how far you are from the line separating your lane from the intersection. However, there might be cult-like factions with people of varying dissents on how far you had to be from the light to slow down or to speed up. Yet, another doctrine might ensue that focuses on how big the intersection is.

These events that could follow outcomes around an intersection with traffic lights are not unlike what we experience with our exercises on what is metaphysical. There is really only one conclusion that I could be drawn. We are really left with two things, what is useful and what is a belief?

So, there are thoughts that we should think, an endless list of them. There are ideas that we must test for whether they hold water. This is my idea of metaphysics.

When I sat down to write some articles on the issue of guns, the issue of abortion, and whether a woman should wear fake hair, my standard for what I had to say, for the way I respectfully wanted to look at these issues as I continued to examine my position was based on what would prevail, what would prove permanent.

Here are two of the articles:

SOCIAL MIND EXERCISE: WOMEN AND FAKE HAIR

I know a young lady who is the quintessence of female pulchritude. My bias aside, consensus, I am confident, has to be that she is indeed 'very easy on the eyes.' She is statuesque at 5 feet 11 inches with those classic features of the Caribbean woman. Of course, this successful young lady's physical attributes pale when I think of her gentle spirit and how she not only put herself through college working as a babysitter (I still do not know how this was possible) but also through a graduate master of business administration degree. In this world of questionable values and reality television, in this culture that looks for a quick solution and little or no sacrifice, this woman is an obvious opposite. To me, she is a god. I regard her as one, that is, until she puts on a wig. When this young lady is not wearing her hair naturally, however, slightly, she becomes ordinary. I feel like she has lowered herself in comparison to everything else that makes her who she is. It leaves me puzzled as to why a person would want to wear fake hair.

This article is not about what is right and what is wrong. If a person decided to wear fake hair, it would not be the end of the world. This article, however, is about what is possible, and that is not a simple thing. The sort of world we could create by pondering our options about anything, in this case, whether wearing fake hair serves us well, is a very demanding exercise for the mind. A good place to start is to know that a strenuous exercise is an option that a person could decide to take on. Just like a person might not want to work out because he found it uncomfortable, a person might choose to work out. Further, a person might choose to go from an exercise with a minimal degree of difficulty to one that is more difficult to endure. In each case, an outcome is created. An outcome is created when we decide to manufacture and place value on fake hair.

One of the most difficult things that any of us would have to wrestle with in a life time is whether a person accepts how he or she looks. It is about what we have convinced one another is the standard for beauty. I am saying all this because I have made the reckless assumption that the reason a person would want to put on fake hair had to be to enhance her looks. What I see, however, is that the idea of what is beautiful is already a struggle within each of us. This struggle is one that we may find is not for the eyes, but rather for the mind. Just like a person who goes to the gym may not be able to lift objects of a certain weight until he exercises his body, some objects may not be easy on the eyes until those eyes' mind is exercised. The eyes are not the struggle. The mind is. Just like a person may find it too burdensome what needs to be known about another person and therefore may resort to stereotype as a shortcut, the eyes are only the easy way out. So if the reason a person puts on a wig is because of what she sees with her eyes, the question is what can she see with herself mind?

A person might live his life by a list of what he could and could not eat. This person might be convinced that what he ate determined what he thought. Another person, on the other hand, might be convinced that what he ate had nothing to do with his idea of virtue and his heart and how he saw and treated his neighbor. Similarly, a person might think that the way to show love would be to tell his spouse everyday that he loved her. He might even have a tradition where he left fresh roses on her night stand every morning. He might be convinced that this was how to convey his love; and she might be eternally fulfilled with these gestures. However, this act would be like a person who thought that the way to keep his heart 'pure' was to be sure to wash his hands before he used them to put anything in his mouth. Like a person whose vision is separated by a foggy screen; this great devotion is one that a person would have to ask himself if it were the real thing. If it turns out that a person did not wish to know if the everyday roses had anything to do with a person's commitment or devotion or faithfulness, there is nothing any of us could do about it. This is an exercise that the person would have to take on by herself. If she did not take on this exercise, it would not be the end of the world only she would not know what is possible.

Is it the best we can do? Is it necessary for us to manufacture a crisis that causes a little girl in a remote part of the world to be exploited by a fake hair entrepreneur? Of course, you might say that a person's life has always been at risk because of what he has in his possession. To this, I say, yes. That is why I have made the claim that the reason we act the way we do is that we are not intelligent enough to act otherwise. That a person's life has always been at risk is perhaps a condition a different sort of mind could alter. Is it necessary to manufacture a reason for one friend to be able to imply to her friend that she is doing better because of the brand of artificial hair she can afford? Is this the only outcome that we are capable of creating? Ultimately, I do not see this article as a lighthearted commentary on fancy social issues. This article is about the conflicts of the human mind – which, by the way, are not wholly multifaceted. This is about how man answers the existential question: Should I do whatever I want just because I can? It is the part that each of us plays. There is a world that is created by the values we espouse. There is an outcome that we have to live with. In this case, it is how a person answers the question when he looks at himself in the mirror: what makes me beautiful?

I have not written this article to provide you with an admonition for what you should think about an issue. It is not my place. That is something that we all have to do on our own. Besides, if I had written this article with the presupposition that I had things figured out, I might be seriously shortchanging myself. What I do hope, however, is that you take on the challenge inherent and see if you would come up with a different thought tomorrow, or a week hereafter, or a year from now; because we could leave things where they are, or we could decide to pursue what is possible.

SOCIAL MIND EXERCISE: THE ISSUE OF GUNS

At any one time, we should be less interested in what a person has to say. I am less interested in what I have to say. These are things that change. What a person has to say can change. Instead, I am more interested in what else a person has to say about what he has said. I would like to see a person take me on a journey, a tour, of his body of work – his body of thought. This must serve as an intellectual framework for the simple fact that the reason we act the way we do is that we are not intelligent enough to act otherwise.

I would like to see a person come back a day after saying something, or a month, or a year, or ten years, after taking a position on an issue, and demonstrate how much more he had thought about that issue. A person would do this by reverently rendering a change of mind or by bringing additional inferences and supporting analogies to show deeper knowledge of his position. This effort is necessary for any of us to show commitment, not to a desire to be right, but rather to the burden of finding what works, what obtains.

It is in this spirit that I attempt to tackle any issue of the day. Hopefully, none of us wakes up in the morning knowing that what drives him is the thought of how many ways he thinks that he is better than his neighbor, or that his ideas are better. My point here is that a serious person is too burdened to care that he is right because he is aware that he may not be. Instead, he just presses on by constantly questioning himself. This is a quality that benefits one, and all, greatly.

In considering the issue of guns, let us use a certain intellectual framework. The framework is comprised of three thought tests: A Useful starting point, A Constant Internal Dialogue, and A Matter of What Is Possible. The point is for a person to be able to say of proposals to any issue that needs resolution, "Is this a useful starting point?" Let me give you an example. One day at work I asked why we did not change the trash, and a person said that it was because we were out of trash bags. In this situation, it is a problem to be out of trash bags, but this should not prevent a person from changing the trash if the person's useful starting point is: We cannot let trash overrun the trash bin. Furthermore, a person should continue an internal dialogue long after he thinks that he has an answer per chance he might find more desirable resolutions; per chance he might find what else is possible.

So in this matter, we should find a USEFUL STARTING POINT. I submit to you that our useful starting point has to be the admission that the way to achieve 'safe' could not be when we each carried a gun on us. The way to create a safe environment for a six-year-old to go for studies is not when there is an armed guard around every corner. The way that a person should feel safe in his home could not be that he slept with his finger on the trigger. If a person has to do this, he has already lost in his desire to be safe. He is already living in a different outcome.

Further in this matter, we should acknowledge unconditionally that if we continued to think long and hard about this matter, and we each engaged in INTERNAL DIALOGUE by not looking at a position that we had taken as an end, our minds might find new and fresh thoughts on how to deal with it. A perspective that comes to mind as a result of my internal dialogue on how to look at the issue of guns in society and hence how to ponder what solution is desirable is this: I could not imagine that triumph belongs to the person who shoots everything up. It is those who laid down their arms that we commend or remember. Bravery is for the person who comes unarmed and not for the person who is armed to the teeth – that is fear.

I was walking down the street late one night, and I thought that the person who was approaching in the other direction looked suspicious. I thought about a number of things. First, I wished that I had a gun so that I could feel safe. I also thought that I could cross over to the other side of the street. But then, I also thought that I felt the way I did only because I was afraid for my life. And then I thought it was interesting that the worth that I placed on my life was that I had to be alive. Hence the reason I saw the person approaching as a threat.

Finally, in the matter, I realize that the conditions in which I find myself – the thoughts that I think, the social issues that I try to resolve, the life that I lead – is an experiment in WHAT IS POSSIBLE. Interestingly, I realized that it was more cowardly of me to think that I could define what is possible in this world, or my world, based solely on whether I stayed alive.

The issue of guns is not a right and wrong one regardless of what position any of us may hold. It is, however, a matter of what is possible. Whatever belief we hold will result in one of two possibilities: will a country become safer or will a country's soul become wearier within her? Our actions will result in whether a kid goes to school and thinks more about the guns around her and less about the possibilities of what is inside the pages of a book; or less about guns and more about the love to learn.

So, there is no right and there is no wrong, just how much more any of us is prepared to ponder the matter at hand because our actions, every single one of them create a world. We just have to ask ourselves if we have thought about what is possible.

The only thought to entertain as human beings, the only exercise in which to engage is one that involves things that last more than a day, or a month, or a year, or ten. All things considered, we should only pursue ideals that stand the test of time. How do we know which ideals stand the test of time? That is the reason I wrote a book. We could try to know it. We do not have to, but we could. If a person decided that what would make him happy is a fleet of cars, there is absolutely nothing that we could do about it. Now, if it turns out that this same individual would only become miserable and depressed five years later, and worse, that his possessions would have something to do with it, could his mind have created a different outlook, one that would not change? Could a person convince himself otherwise, early on, so that he would not find when he went home at night, and the next night, and ten years later, and when he is dying, what he thought of all the cars he owned?

OUR TEST FOR WHAT IS METAPHYSICAL IS WHAT STANDS THE TEST OF TIME. THIS IS THE ONLY THING THAT IS USEFUL. THIS IS THE ONLY THING THAT OBTAINS.

THE BARACK OBAMA JUNCTURE

6 ON KNOWING

The reason we act the way we do is that we are not intelligent enough to act otherwise.

In this light, any conversation or questioning that may develop on the subject of knowledge, what it is and how we acquire it, remains as a subscript in the sense that at the end of the day, it would not matter how we acquired knowledge. It would only matter that we did.

My position is not to trivialize any value that may be accorded to our devotion to the study of what is knowable and how it is that we come to know. However, its relevance only rises to the level of importance that one might place on trying to discover if a person acquires strength and conditioning through weight training or through plyometrics.

My idea of epistemology is not that a person can define for me what knowledge is. The chances of that becoming an epiphany is at the level of a camera finding out that it sees with a lens. It is also at the level of a person discovering what it means to be strong, or being able to pose the question, 'what is strength?' My idea of epistemology is not whether I know but rather whether what I know is useful.

Epistemology is the work it takes for a person to make certain that what he has known is what to know.

My point is this: It is admirable for a person to want to ask himself questions about the origin and limits of human knowledge. He may want to ask, "How is it that I know what I know?" He may become consumed by this. He may want to spend his time on methods to JUSTIFY what it is that he claims to know. This is remarkable only if the question he hopes to answer is, "How do I know what I know?" However, if he considers the 'then what,' where does that leave his idea of epistemology? Where does he go with his epistemological quest?

If a Canon camera finds out how it works, then what? What will it do with that bit of information? If a tree finds out how it gets water, to what end will it use that information? If somehow man finds out that it is his ability for perception that makes it all make sense for him, then what? If it is the case that introspection and memory and reason assure him of what he claims to know, would it then be settled?

The quest for how a person comes to know what he knows is a noble one. A more useful preoccupation, however, is what does a person do with what it is that he can know, or rather what does he do with his ability to know things? My idea of **Useful Philosophy** is not for us to dwell on speculations, or even what might be obvious, but rather what we do with a nature that is already there. What good does it do the blossom if it does not turn toward the light?

I think that one of the most compelling things that any of us could learn comes from the little-known Nike slogan: Just Do It. Not to draw attention to myself but what I learned from having been an athlete did not come from playing soccer – I had room for error there. As a hundred meter sprinter of clearly world class outfitting, however, I had a different experience. Forget the training, forget coaching, forget dedication and commitment and focus that I could seek in varying degrees, when it was time for me to run I had other thoughts going on in my head. I could not just do it. It is where the phrase, Just Do It, becomes so fitting. I am sure that this is what Nike had in mind. What use is there if we spend a lifetime analyzing how we do what we do yet when it comes time to display those skills and knowledge toward anything that matters, we are nowhere to be found?

I do not find that the question Usain Bolt wakes up asking himself every morning is, "How is it that I can run so speedily?" He does not give his time to the study of skeleton and muscle and what these are, primarily. I suspect that he wakes up building on his assurance that he indeed is a speedster by continuing to understand the mechanics of running fast. He does not devote his resources to asking himself and employing the service of the rest of the world in helping him answer the question, 'how do I know that I can run fast or what is it to run fast?'

An analogy that comes to mind in trying to sort out my thoughts on what to make of knowledge and knowing involves businesses. Not that long ago, may be as recently as twenty-five years, a corporation might have looked at an employee and acknowledge that he was good at what he did. There were corporations a good while ago with thought and value processes that focused on who demonstrated what skill or to what degree a particular skill was demonstrated.

In recent times, of course, somebody obviously thought that it should matter less to a corporation how skilled an individual is, and that it should matter more that an associate can make the people he works with better at what they do – that a person finds sharing what he knows more important than what he knows. That is, somebody eventually thought that it would not matter how good one person is on a basketball team of five players because it would take all five of them to win a game.

It should matter less how a person knows what he knows. It should be of greater focus that what is known is what to know. We could spend more time focused on bridging the gap between what we know and what to know. I find this to be more useful than dwelling on thoughts that potentially go nowhere.

One day at work, I needed to show an associate how to complete a task. When I finished explaining what essentially is the first stage of a three or four layer process, the associate said, "I've got it." So, there I was, needing to tell my associate that I was not done explaining the process in its entirety. Essentially, if we had stopped when the person said, "I've got it," it would have become evident that what the person knew was not what to know. I certainly would have preferred that this individual spent time on this priority, and not on anything else like 'do I really know what I was just told? Is it because I heard it, or because I was shown?'

Since the reason we act the way we do is that we are not intelligent enough to act otherwise, there is a level of incongruity in the idea of epistemology as we currently know it. As a result, it would be useful to reconsider what we may have thought of its definition in the first place.

Again, the idea of wanting to know if we acquire knowledge through divine intervention, or our senses, or other methods, is like wanting to know if a person becomes strong and conditioned by lifting weights or through plyometrics. It is a focus that potentially does not obtain. It is unlikely that one would find that it is one method or the other. If there is any truth to this as legitimate methods, of knowledge acquisition, it would be that they simply are tools.

For this reason, I find that our exercise should be toward what is useful to us – what we can use. Like an associate who may find that there is more to know, our studies should be on how a person gets to an 'I understand it' stage. This could be a consuming but useful engagement. There are enough thoughts that we could spend our time sorting out that would create tremendously useful outcomes for society. We should do this at every juncture by posing the question, 'Do I know what I have known?' Another way to ask this question is, 'Is what I know what I am supposed to know?'

A young guy who becomes a professional basketball player is having so much money dumped into his lap than he has ever seen before, an incomprehensible amount of money. This man, in a moment of lust, or his perpetual moments of lust, realizes that with his new status and means, he could afford most things. He realizes that he could even afford a woman, the way he dreamed of her. So he calls up the woman he would want to be with. He finds out that he could have her for $20,000. He does not mind. He could afford it, relatively speaking.

So the woman who gets called up to entertain a man's wild dreams could not help but think to herself, "I am this influential. I must be important. Forget everyone who has ever worked hard for anything, anyone who has toiled for something. If I can make $20,000 in one night, I must be important." So she thinks this and she brags about it. She tells everybody to go to hell. She has money. This is currency. This is leverage.

Now, there is a man who is barely able to put food on the table for his family. He goes to the game. He scrapes money together to give his family a good life, including taking his young son to the basketball game from time to time. We could speculate about how much he pays for the tickets, and how often he can take his darling son to the game to spend valuable time with him. Of course, it would not be a stretch to think that there is correlation between the cost of a ticket and how much players are paid. In any case, the proud father reminds his son every chance he gets to work diligently, to study hard, and to make a difference. He convinces his son that dreams do become reality.

The boy sees all this and thinks, "What I need to do is find a way to live like this basketball player even though I do not know how to play basketball." He goes on to think, "This is amazing. I want to be able to put myself in a position where I can fulfill every desire, every impulse. I can look at a girl whom I want and actually get her. It would be unlike the dreams that I have now that I am unable to attain once I wake up. I can make this dream reality."

So here is my point: Who gets to tell that boy and the rest of us how a guy who bounces a basketball around a court is worth more than his father? Who gets to tell him that a person who opens up her legs to cater to the indulgences of others is in command of the outcomes that we could use to sustain the future? Who gets to tell him that he might not want to live by lust and desires alone but by control and denials as well? Who may want to tell him that if his father paid less for the tickets every time they went to the game, his future might be a little more secure?

The questions in this context are this: Is what the young fellow knows of the life of his basketball playing role model what is to know? Further, is the way the player sees things, is what he has known, what to know? There is a young man who seemingly now has two gaps to bridge. This is a useful starting point. This is my idea of epistemology. Please, do not get me wrong. Everyone is fine the way he is. I have not written this book to criticize anyone's position or values. If a person wants to spend the weekend at a brothel and pick out every woman of his desire and indulge himself unconscious, or dead, this would be perfectly fine. No judgement. I have written this book so that we could ask ourselves at any one time, of any one thing we are doing, if we can imagine what else is possible for us, for others.

I wrote an article a while back about how I thought running a business is like being on a date. Here is the article:

The earliest memories that I have of 'boy meets girl' is when my sister, who is older, would come home from school and all that she did was talk about this guy in her class. Every other word out of her mouth was his name. When she started dating him, the way she felt about this man only intensified. She could not wait to see him. She looked forward to spending time with him. She talked about him with anyone who would grant her an audience. And then one day, all of it stopped. I do not believe she mentioned his name ever again. This experience and others have prompted me to conclude that running a business is like being on a date. How?

Running a business involves real relationships. It is important to know categorically that the same people who talk about how wonderful your business is can one day stop talking about you completely. They may even take the time to talk very unfavorably about you. I want you to be able to read between the lines here because this is an article and not a book on how to run your business from day to day. My point is that your business is not going to be perfect, but you can achieve having your patrons look at you perfectly. Of course, as with a relationship, there are actions that can make a person who has thought the world of you suddenly develop a proverbial bad taste in the mouth. In other words, even if a client decides to 'see other people,' you have to be 'cool' about it. You cannot afford the breakup to be irreparable because every single day that there is a person who has nothing good to say about you, your business suffers.

You have to put in an effort. Before you got all cleaned up and got all stylish, before you started wearing Kenneth Cole boots, nobody noticed you. You knew the caliber of people that you could attract, if anyone talked to you, at all. Of course, your chances of approaching someone else's girlfriend and convincing her that she could do better was definitely zero, a joke. However, this changed. It changed in that people began to notice you – your business. People wanted to 'check you out.' So, you went from a person no one cared to spend time with to a person more and more people looked forward to having around. As a result, because you were doing something right, it got better for you. You made enough changes and as a result you could go out and compete. You could approach business accounts and take them away from your competitors. You went from a person who just sat there hoping that somebody talked to him to a person who now could say, "That girl with the most popular guy at the school, I am going to talk to her and steal her from him."

Running a business is not about a person. With a big target on your back, you have gone from someone to whom people paid no attention to someone of whom people said, "I want what he has." You have found yourself with the reality that you have to work to keep what you have. You realized very quickly that you needed to get rid of the word familiarity. Let me explain what I mean because a lot of people get confused and ask me questions like, "Are you saying we should not talk to customers anymore?" No, this is not what I mean. What I am saying is that when you are familiar with something, you take it for granted. So, let me introduce you to a word: PROPERSONAL. This means that you conduct yourself in a professional and personal way. What I am saying is that when you were dating a person, you did not leave dishes in the sink overnight because she was the clean type, but then she became 'yours,' and you could not keep the house clean any longer. Of course, one day, because familiarity can breed contempt, she, often without ever giving you a list of everything that you did not bother to handle with dignity anymore – wait, I meant PROPERSONALLY – she packed up and went somewhere else. What I am saying is that your sweet spot is when your customer can say, "I have fun with those people. I feel like I know them, but I still get the high level of service and effort that they genuinely displayed the first time I became their patron."

In business you have to be predictable. You may have heard the term that business has to be predictable. This is true. One day I am at work having a fantastic day when a representative from a local coffee company stopped by to sell their services. Because I am impressionable, we set up a date for a demonstration. The day came and the representative never showed. Days later, I emailed him just out of curiosity and fairness that he may have been ill. He replied to my email with an apology and a new appointment except, he did not show up again. I could not help but jokingly think, like a person who is stood up on a date, "Is it me – what is wrong with me?" Of course, what I learned from the experience was that I could not do business – be in a relationship – with a company that I could not predict. It simply is not going to work if you cannot say, "I have an idea what is going to happen next." The people who do business with you have to be able to trust that certain things about your business are a surety. That is cool. That is sexy. That is character. That is respect.

Run your business with intentionality. Most people still either do not know this or do not yet agree that the reason a person would not become unfaithful to his spouse is not because he loved her. There are enough examples of people who in spite of their professed love for their spouses did transgressed. How do we know this? We know this because we have heard people say it while in their state of regret and remorse. Clearly, the one thing that outweighs love is a persons understanding of the commitment that he, not while under duress, made to another person. Run your business like a person who really values the word he gives. This will help you demonstrate sound judgment. It will also be the impetus for how much you try to know about your business, how much more knowledge you try to gather and expertise you try to develop in your business environment. A person who can achieve a level of precision in the way he handles business because he is familiar with the situation is also the person who is not going to be confused about what his choices mean if he finds himself in a compromising situation.

Finally, you have to be able to compartmentalize. In life, as in business, there is a season for everything. Simply, there is a time for everything. There is a time for a person to think about his children, and there is a time not to. There is a time to fiddle with your smart phone, and there is a time not to. There is a time to look at Facebook, and there is a time not to. As with relationship, there is cost when things are done out of order, or when things are done at inappropriate times. When gratification is not delayed or discipline is shunned, there is chaos. In 2005, people displaced by Hurricane Katrina would soon make their way as far up as Huntsville, Alabama. As a hotel operator, I was faced with renting rooms to people who may have lost everything. This was before it became clear that The American Red Cross was going to pay for the accommodation of those affected. We had to choose between looking at the people who came through our doors as destitute individuals who needed help, or simply as people who needed a place to lay their heads. At that juncture, I had to tell myself that I was a hotel operator, not the director of a non-profit or the nicest and most generous human being on the face of the earth. I sold rooms to people, sometimes to people who did not have much to spare. So, we did the best that we could on room rates and provided the best service that we could, including putting these guests in touch with various organizations and individuals in the community who were already organizing to lend a hand. At the time, I knew another hotel operator who did the exact opposite. This individual showed 'more care' than I did. In fact, we joked about how 'cold heart' I was. However, in a matter of days, my colleague's hotel was not a hotel anymore; it was a drop zone where people brought food and clothing. While I was running a hotel, my colleague was running a shelter. Needless to say that it became unfair to the other guests who were not there because of Hurricane Katrina.

Running a business is a humbling experience. It is an endless field of opportunity to test ideas and justify them – a place to learn what works and what does not. Running a business presents an infinite supply of analogies and ways of seeing things that are easily transposed to other areas of life. The idea of looking at running a business as if it were a dating engagement is perhaps the most exciting thing that has happened to my work environment. I am as much a student as anyone to whom I may have shared the concept. So far, every new situation that we run into and to which we apply the concept, we have managed to navigate with success.

Of course, the question I will end up asking myself repeatedly is,

"Are all these things that I have said useful?" I will forever wonder if I missed the mark, or if what I have thought is what I should have thought. I find that my time is better spent not pondering how it is that I come to know, or if I know that I know. I find that the dividend for me is in the assurance that what I know is what to know. For anyone who might think at this point, 'what if there isn't anything to know,' the pursuit becomes settling the chances that there really is nothing to know, however trivial.

In order to get to what is possible in this world, we are clearly bound in our thinking by what constitutes a useful starting point, and our internal dialogue, the existence of it, for starters, is the bridge between these two conditions. Our work is not an abstraction. It should not be. Our must reflect an acknowledgement that what is to be known is what to know. THIS IS OUR EPISTEME.

The most profound thoughts that we would ever entertain in our lifetime, in perhaps any lifetime, have happened under the Presidency of Barack Obama. I have said this acknowledging that there is probably nothing new under the sun. If the presidency is simply a juncture that has allowed us to revisit considerations that can be useful to society, then alone in that regard, it is noteworthy. My point, for instance, is that if not for the presidency of Barack Obama, I am not sure that I would have spent much time trying to think about the word COMPROMISE, if not because it has been used so much in the effort for a two-party system to find ways to govern.

My interest of course in what I could know about the word compromise as a result of how I have seen it used and played out in a political process is not focused on the word, or its etymology, or how one particular individual attempts to use it, and if he uses it accurately or appropriately. My interest is whether the people who use the word understand its intended meaning enough to find it as a useful tool or concept for the way they go about carrying out their responsibilities. Is what a person has known what there is to know?

THE BARACK OBAMA JUNCTURE

The way that I see the Barack Obama presidency is similar to the way I would see a person who went out and bought a car that he really loves, a fine piece of automobile. If it turns out that this vehicle that is worth so much actually cannot function in the rain because it does not have wiper blades, or even traction control systems for wet surfaces, the owner may never know this. If it never rains, there are issues about the automobile that our friend may never have to worry about. He may never have to look at himself with regards to his choice of vehicle any differently.

When President Barack Obama made a comment about starting a business and the effort that goes into seeing it succeed, and he said, "You did not build that," implying there are components of a person's success which he did not orchestrate on his own, this became a huge hot-button topic. I thought that this was great for society. I thought that any day that the mind was taken to a different place, the same way a person finds a different exercise to do in the gym, is a day of advancement toward what is possible. Though this was an event that forced me to think about the issue in my own terms, beyond this, any conclusions that I made could not have been improved upon by how I came to make them. In other words, it would not be useful, or maybe even possible, to say, "You know, if I had come to know what I know through a method other than the one I know, I could have thought differently about this issue of whether a person succeeds alone or whether he could coexist with the thought of his genuine sacrifice, and the idea that he could not have done it alone."

One of the things that I have known unequivocally running a hotel operation is that everything has to be about the guest. It is the standard, the compass, for how we conduct ourselves and for how we treat our friend guests. To us, it is like being in a relationship, one that you hope would work out. So, for instance, for any staff member, or two, who may be occupied or may be in an important work related conversation, whenever a guest comes into the picture, the expectation is for the focus and attention to shift immediately to the guest. It is about the guest's needs. That comes first for us in all situations. Everyday, we ask ourselves if the way we go about our business is the way to go about it. We ask ourselves if what we have known about it obtains, if it prevails.

One of the methods that we have adopted at work is that even though we are in a hospitality environment, we are really not trying to be nice to people but rather provide them with service. Cosmetically, it may look like we are a bunch of very nice people. In fact, you could put two businesses side by side and not be able to tell which one thinks its job is to be nice and which one sees being nice as just a product of the service it attempts to provide. You may not see these differences until of course there is a test. The difference between these two dynamics might be as obvious as acknowledging that it might be easier for one person who operates not on trying to accommodate not to promise something that he does not have than it might be for another person who is driven by the need to accommodate.

I love my car. I love everything about my car. As a car enthusiast who spends a lot of time looking at cars and appreciating them, my car is the only car about which I simply have nothing that I would like to redo. With this position that I hold about my car, I realize profoundly that I have very little use for this information for the simple reason that not every car would look like mine. Even if other car companies had similar design approach of a swept forward sports car look with a small front and plenty of road visibility, not every car designed with this in mind would look like mine. Not every car could look the same. Not every human being could be the same. We would not all have the same set of skills. They would be different because we are different. We are good at different things. Knowing this, and knowing that maybe somebody feels the same way about his car as I do about mine, is an example of the exercise for my mind on whether I walk around thinking that my car is nicer than someone else's car; or whether I know that if I could think it, so could others.

I know an individual with means. I recall him say that he did not lay anyone off during a recent economic downturn. Maybe this was a relative thing to say, and some people were let go. Either way, knowing him, the impetus for hanging on to associates in one capacity or another had to be because of concern for their families and means of livelihood. I recognize that there was tremendous cost to making a decision as such. Now as I was thinking this, my mind was eager to conclude that this would not have happened had it been a corporation. That if all the people were working for a corporation, they would have been terminated due to the downturn. While I was thinking this, I did not think that my thought process could not be completely defended or at least that my rationale should be questioned. There was nothing that stops a Corporation from thinking like a Sole Proprietor. I realized that what I was trying to say was that it would be erroneous to think that a person is better off only if he worked for an individual and not a corporation, and vice versa. It is the outcome of either of these two systems that means anything.

One very busy day at my hotel, a regular guest showed up and needed a room. It was one of those special nights and the rate we always gave him was not available. The rate, by the way, was one that we created over the previous few months to move room inventories. It was very successful because people, including our regular guest, took advantage of it.

In any case, on this particular night, we told our friend that the deeply discounted rate was not available. To our amazement, he did not find this acceptable. As a result, we, first my staff, and then myself, spent the next ten minutes trying to explain to the individual why he would have to pay regular rate for the room. More amazing, and irreconcilable, was how combative and entitled the individual made his case for why we should rent a room to him at a rate that we created, the one of which he had taken advantage, and that we had decided for the one day would not be available.

The reason I bring up this story is that I often wonder if our mind is up to the challenge, if we actually know what we are up against, if we recognize the challenge and then start trying to measure up to it.

I thought that the mind of our potential guest was only as curious as that of a person who discovers calculus, begins to master it, and somehow in the middle of that and a new found feel good discovery about himself concludes that there is no God.

Epistemology is the work that it takes a person who has known something to assure himself that he knows that thing, to find out that he knows what he has known. His work is to find out if what he has known is what to know.

I told a person I ran into the other day who was reading the book, The Uncertain Believer: Reconciling God and Science, by Edward Correia, that there was nothing to reconcile. It is not that there is not a level of confidence that begins to bubble when a person goes from wondering about conception and how life comes into being, to being close enough to it by uniting sperm and egg in a petri dish. I get it.

To declare that there is God is a belief that has nothing to do with science. Wait for it. It gets interesting. For one thing, how does a mind that is constantly in the process of discovery declare what it is that is to be discovered?! However, this is not even the point that I am trying to make. The point that I am making is omni-cognitive. I am more interested in the seriousness of the exercise that the mind has to go through to contain the idea of 'belief' or that of 'disbelief' in the same way that I am interested in the working of the mind of the potential guest who had trouble when we told him that we could not sell a room at the rate he wanted.

The idea of whether we think there is a God or not pales in comparison to being able to comprehend that it is a belief. We would need to grasp the concept the same way that we have accepted that the earth is round and that the sun rises from the east. This is an exercise that the mind could find to be very challenging in a way similar to how the guest at the hotel found having to pay a different rate very challenging to accept.

It is as a result of the exercise to which the mind should bequeath itself that it is worth saying that religion is not the issue, a person is.

The reason I have told a bunch of seemingly disjointed stories is that it would be useless of me to absorb myself in nebulous thoughts like, "Am I alive right now?" or "How do I know that I know what I know?" I could engage in thoughts that generate real outcomes. There is enough in front of us. There are more challenges, even immediate one, to overcome. It is no coincidence that this book could as well be summed up in the thought that even when what is appropriate to an end is evident, a human being may tend to do something else. The reason, as we can conclude based on what I have said so far, being that often the appropriate thought weighs more than a person can exercise.

The reason we act the way we do is that we are not intelligent enough to act otherwise. The smallest effort for unceasing dialogue is a useful starting point that will put us closer to what else is possible.

7 NOTES

1. Watch Franklin Graham Question President Obama's Faith, Explain Why Mormons Aren't Christian On Morning Joe. (2012). http://www.mediaite.com/tv/watch-franklin-graham-question-president-obamas-faith-explain-why-mormons-arent-christian-on-morning-joe/
2. Full Transcript: President Barack Obama's Inaugural Address. (2009). http://abcnews.go.com/Politics/Inauguration/president-%20%20obama-inauguration-speech-transcript/story?id=6689022&page=2
3. Congressman Yells 'You Lie' at Obama During Speech. (2009). http://www.foxnews.com/politics/2009/09/10/congressman-yells-lie-obama-speech/
4. Obama's problem? No one fears him. (2011). http://www.cnn.com/2011/OPINION/09/02/martin.obama.power/index.html

5. Truth and Reconciliation. (2004). http://greatergood.berkeley.edu/article/item/truth_and_reconciliation
6. Transcript: Obama address to U.N. General Assembly. (2012). http://www.foxnews.com/politics/2012/09/25/transcript-obama-address-to-un-general-assembly/
7. Mourdock: Compromise is Democrats Agreeing With Republicans. (2012). http://news.yahoo.com/mourdock-compromise-democrats-agreeing-republicans-080209091.html
8. N.C. Preacher Tells Parents to Crack Wrists, Punch Effeminate Children. (2012). http://www.advocate.com/society/religion/2012/05/01/north-carolina-pastor-advocates-punching-gay-acting-children
9. Supreme Court Justice Ruth Bader Ginsberg snubs the U. S. Constitution. (2012). http://www.livinglakecountry.com/blogs/communityblogs/139051714.html
10. Pat Robertson Claims God 'Showed' Him Who The Next President Will Be. (2012). http://www.theblaze.com/stories/2012/01/04/pat-robertson-claims-god-showed-him-who-the-next-president-will-be/Daily Show Hijacks Rick Scott Presser: Prove You're Not On Drugs By Peeing In This Cup. (2011). http://tpmmuckraker.talkingpointsmemo.com/2011/12/daily_show_hijacks_rick_scott_presser_prove_youre.php

11. Mark Zuckerberg. (2010). http://www.time.com/time/specials/packages/article/0,28804,2036683_2037183_2037185-1,00.html
12. Ibid
13. Ibid
14. How The Tech Boom Went Bust. (2002). http://www.businessweek.com/stories/2002-02-24/how-the-tech-boom-went-bust
15. The Colbert Report. (2011). http://www.colbertnation.com/the-colbert-report-videos/394151/august-08-2011/nassir-ghaemi
16. String of Pearls by Michael Franks. (1993). http://www.superlyrics.com/lyrics/kGRU0hgGZ0@H@j/String_Of_Pearls_lyrics_by_Michael_Franks.html

www.ingramcontent.com/pod-product-compliance
Lightning Source LLC
Chambersburg PA
CBHW070809100426
42742CB00012B/2313